"The format works so well because it instructs through answering questions submitted by real people seeking advice. I thoroughly enjoyed *The Practical Negotiator* and highly recommend it to anyone who wishes to improve his or her negotiating skills."

—Earl Hill, Senior Lecturer, Emory University, Goizueta Business School

"...a valuable addition for all of us whose tool kit is a bit light on conciliation skills—and that's most of us."

—Justine Hardy, author of *The Wonder House* and *In the Valley of Mist* and founder of the conflict rehabilitation program Healing Kashmir

"This straightforward and nicely nuanced book lives up to its practical title. The chapter headings help to organize the book to make it a useful guide for a wide variety of people. The question-and-answer format makes the information approachable. Mr. Cohen's development of detailed answers to sometimes difficult questions is enhanced by his business experience and good psychological awareness. His background as a lawyer adds substantially to his creative answers to complicated problems. His approach is especially helpful for the non-legally-trained. His varied suggestions for each problem encourage the reader to be open-minded."

—Sylvia Topp, PhD, clinical psychologist

"*The Practical Negotiator* will better arm everyone for whatever life throws his or her way. The real-life questions submitted from every corner of the planet make for a fascinating read and underscore [the fact] that everything in life is a negotiation. With his prodigious knowledge and laser-like insights, Steven Cohen masterfully dissects every situation to the core and systematically shows us how to construct a solution. It's like having a consultant and mentor at your side. I recommend you read *The Practical Negotiator* straight through, then keep it at your fingertips for frequent reference."

—Joe Grimaldi, Chairman & CEO, Mullen Advertising

"If you've ever wondered how the win-win approach to negotiation plays out in the real world, here is the perfect guide. With authority, verve, and extraordinary range, Steve Cohen walks us through dozens and dozens of actual negotiations. Based on his world-wide practice of several decades, he introduces us to real people with real problems—in business, in leisure pursuits, in personal life—and then analyzes and advises. His cool head and warm heart make him an excellent teacher. Fascinating, engaging, and extremely useful."

—Miriam Weinstein, author, *The Surprising Power of Family Meals*

"In this highly entertaining and instructive book, the author draws on his background in law and decades of experience in writing about and teaching the art of negotiation. Answering a variety of real-life questions posed by individuals from around the globe, Mr. Cohen teaches by _____ ___ht of his sense of humor. Topics analyzed and discussed range fr_____ss negotiations to maintaining peace and harmony with t]_____vice and constructive food for thought, the book ulti-r_____ndamentals of successful negotiation and reminds us that €_____verful and transformative tool."

—Ann____ ____rtified Genetic Counselor, Medical City Dallas Hospital

"Steve Cohen has created an interesting and useful read. As a medical doctor, every aspect of my day-to-day interactions with my patients, their relatives, and my colleagues involves careful attention to negotiation style. Whilst not directly related to this, the examples and advice he provides can be extrapolated to almost any scenario. The style is direct, unpretentious, and clear, [and] geared toward people with experience in this field but also lay folk such as myself. It is written in such as way as to reinforce key concepts and encourage thought and further reading [on] the subject, facilitating an essential learning experience for anyone who negotiates on a daily basis—which I suspect is everyone!"

—Dr. Luke Morgan-Rowe, SpR Radiology, The Royal Free London

"*The Practical Negotiator* is an incredibly helpful guide to getting what you want and feel you deserve. Cohen provides thoughtful responses to many questions I've asked myself and scenarios I've contemplated as I navigate the early stages of my career. In my personal life, I can see myself referring back to *The Practical Negotiator* as I make decisions and seek to influence positive outcomes for my relationships, family, and financial well-being."

—Olivia Kerr, government relations communications manager in Washington, D.C.

"Leadership in emergency services is a matter of having people trust your judgment. You learn to issue commands that help volunteers feel that they have been involved in the process. It is a skill I've refined by reading *The Practical Negotiator*."

—Terry Kemper, captain, East Hampton, N.Y. volunteer fire department

"There are books you read once and leave, and there are those you keep referring to. *The Practical Negotiator* is the latter. It beautifully captures what most of us go through in our personal and professional lives, and is a great reckoner; hence [it] has high longevity on your shelf."

—Rachna Chhachhi, nutritional therapist specializing in management and reversal of chronic lifestyle diseases without medication

"Reading through Steven P. Cohen's *The Practical Negotiator*, I was struck by the forthrightness of the text, and by his reliance on words such as *honesty* and *respect*, and the emphasis on seeing negotiation as...cooperation toward a mutual identified goal, rather than as a competition defining a winner and loser. And through it all, Mr. Cohen puts forward a concept much in use by educators everywhere: that of *approximations toward a goal*. The idea is that one arrives at one's destination through a series of intermediate acts, not by introducing ultimata or by presenting the final product on a take-it-or-leave-it basis. The author insists throughout that a negotiator be prepared and knowledgeable, in regard to both his/her needs and of those of the opponent. Such thorough preparation helps to move those previously cited intermediate steps along, and promotes a sense of honest discussion in the process. Certainly worth a read for anyone involved in negotiating his/her future."

—Willie Lorsung, retired Minneapolis public school teacher

# THE PRACTICAL NEGOTIATOR

## HOW TO ARGUE YOUR POINT, PLEAD YOUR CASE, AND PREVAIL IN ANY SITUATION

By Steven P. Cohen

CAREER
PRESS

Pompton Plains, NJ

THE PRACTICAL NEGOTIATOR
EDITED BY KIRSTEN DALLEY
TYPESET BY DIANA GHAZZAWI
Cover design by Ian Shimkoviak/theBookDesigners
Printed in the U.S.A.

To order this title, please call toll-free 1-800-CAREER-1 (NJ and Canada: 201-848-0310) to order using VISA or MasterCard, or for further information on books from Career Press.

The Career Press, Inc.
220 West Parkway, Unit 12
Pompton Plains, NJ 07444
www.careerpress.com

Library of Congress Cataloging-in-Publication Data

CIP Data Available Upon Request

To Andréa F. F. MacLeod

# Acknowledgments

I have learned about the practical use of negotiation from fantastic clients, terrific students, my daughters, Julia and Abigail, and my father, the late Martin E. Cohen. As well, help from my assistants, the late Felicity F. Hoyt, Marsha M. Vaughan, and Jennifer P. Whitney, has been invaluable in the writing of this book. I would also like to thank my editor, Kirsten Dalley, for her invaluable help in developing the content and creating a polished final product.

# Contents

# Preface

Like virtually everyone else in the world, I have been negotiating all my life. Whether it was trying to convince my parents to let me stay up later, representing Boston as the city's Washington lobbyist, working on leases for my family's commercial real estate firm, or trying to convince my own children that it was time to go to bed, the process of collaborative decision-making has been a constant.

In more than two decades as a negotiation mentor and trainer for corporate clients, students, and everyday people from more than 85 countries, I have been asked for advice about how to negotiate in an incredible variety of situations. Even before I first visited India, a Web magazine aimed at Indian women recruited me as their advice columnist. After my own firm, The Negotiation Skills Company, added an Advice section to its Website, hundreds of people from around the world sent in negotiation advice questions. All of the questions I received taught me that, fundamentally, people everywhere face similar problems—on the job, as consumers, as neighbors, and with family and friends. This book contains scores of negotiation questions that real people have sent me, as well as the responses I have offered to them. The underlying aim of each is to open your mind to the broad range of choices that should be considered as you attempt to reach agreement with others.

Each question in this book was submitted by a real person looking for advice. Except for corrections to increase clarity or protect privacy, what you see is the question as it arrived in my inbox.

Welcome to the real world of practical negotiation!

Steven P. Cohen

Pride's Crossing, Massachusetts

August, 2013

# Introduction

People often think of negotiation as something that is conducted by political leaders behind closed doors at international summits, or as a kind of antagonistic wheeling and dealing hashed out by corporate chiefs/bullies. These are certainly opportunities for negotiation, but far more negotiation takes place in the daily life of average people who are trying to reach collaborative agreement in the family unit, on the job, or as part of their activities as consumers. Taking a collaborative approach to negotiation increases the likelihood participants will buy in to the ultimate agreement. Treating other negotiators as partners means "we're in this together."

Negotiation may well be crucial in the making of history, but it is also a fundamental aspect of everyday life. The questions in this book originated from real people all around the world and cover a huge range of normal human activity. In the real world, we are all negotiators. We negotiate daily with family and friends, at work, and in the daily business of life. Within this universal endeavor, however, there exist a multitude of possible styles and approaches, based on the particular people involved and what is being negotiated. Styles can vary depending on a broad range of factors, including cultural background, gender, and age. We also tend to view certain kinds of people as being more likely to have a particular, characteristic negotiation style—for example, certain well-known tactics probably come to mind when you think of used car salespeople or the bureaucrats at the local Motor Vehicles agency.

No matter who you are or what is at stake, when you negotiate, your choices will be guided by your answers to certain key questions, such as:

- What do I need to learn to be well-prepared to negotiate?

- Who or what is most likely to solve the problem?

- What information do I need from my negotiation partner that will help me know whether we're heading in a favorable direction?

- When is it time to walk away? What lines need to be crossed before I will do so? What are my dealbreakers—the issues that make it more appropriate to quit negotiating?

- How can I be confident my negotiation partner will fulfill his or her promises?

As you read through the book, you'll find that there are many more questions you'll need to ask yourself; the important thing is to be prepared to do so.

The negotiation process is essentially a way to reach agreement by focusing on the interests of all parties. That said, understanding interests is not merely a matter of identifying your own or another party's objectives (although it is that, too), but also of figuring out *why* achieving each objective is important. In Japan, good negotiators ask what are called the "Five Whys" to get to the heart of this very important issue. For example: *Why is this objective important? What favorable results will it yield? If those results are achieved, what good will it do? What other ways of achieving these favorable results might be better? If there is one factor that is most likely to drive my/their decision, what is it?* Although these questions can take many forms—as you can see, they don't even need to begin with "why"—ultimately the aim here is to find out what, exactly, is driving the decisions of each negotiator.

As you read the rest of the book, you'll see that there are some important guiding principles you'll need to keep top-of-mind:

- Successful negotiation is a process that leads to an agreement each party will willingly fulfill.

- Understanding one's own interests is the first step in preparing for negotiation.

- Never give away one of your interests without deriving a reward for doing so. What you give away is virtually impossible to get back.

- Negotiation is not a competitive sport. If a party concludes that she has lost in a negotiation, she is more likely to avoid fulfilling her commitments and attempt to weasel out of the deal. Conversely, the "winning" negotiator may find that the presumptive gains from the negotiation are not achieved and the net result is failure for both parties.

- Always look for your BATNA—your Best Alternative to a Negotiated Agreement. This will come into play when you're deciding whether to continue negotiating or to walk away.

- Use your information-gathering skills to understand the ZOPA—Zone of Possible Agreement, or the range of possible solutions that will yield an agreement. That way, you're not limiting yourself by fixating on *the* one solution.

People refer to negotiation variously as an art, a science, a natural-born talent, or a skill that can be learned. The reality is that negotiation is all of the above and a lot more. No matter how adept you may be, you can always learn new skills—unless, of course, you are four years old and always get your way!

To make this book easier to use as a reference, I've grouped all of the questions and answers under general topics. Because of the complex nature of some of the queries, however, very often an issue raised in one chapter will appear in another, as well. As often as possible, I've proffered multiple choices of strategies or tactics for handling the problem. Choosing among these options is a personal choice that each negotiator must make independently.

People everywhere have an urgent need to represent themselves with creativity and consciousness in order to make their daily lives run more smoothly. It's my hope that this book will do just that for you, too.

# Chapter 1

# The Basics:
# Some Guidelines and Strategies

---

## Theories of Negotiation

### From: Pablo, Manchester, UK

**Question:** *I would like to know if there are any theories of negotiation.*

**Response:** There are indeed many approaches people use when negotiating. Generally speaking the choices can be described using four Cs.

The first pair of Cs are Confrontational or Competitive. In each case, negotiators are aiming to win; they view the negotiation process as a zero sum game. Confrontational or Competitive negotiation can lead to a variety of negative consequences; the worst is war. Even in more peaceful situations, if a party feels she has "lost" a negotiation, her motivation to fulfill the agreement is substantially reduced; as a consequence, the long-term gains of the "winner" may be less than he wishes.

The other pair of Cs are Collaborative or Cooperative. In this approach, negotiation is viewed as a means for two or more parties to work together to achieve an agreement that is mutually acceptable. There are far greater odds that this approach will lead to shared long-term gains and an agreement that is fulfilled. That is the ultimate test of whether negotiation has worked.

## How Do Personal Characteristics or Attitudes Affect Negotiation?

### From: Fahad, Kuwait City, Kuwait

**Question:** *How do personal characteristics or attitudes affect negotiation?*

**Response:** At the risk of sounding overly simplistic, personality and attitude are extremely significant factors in negotiation—to some people. To others, those two issues might be less significant. An old friend of mine said, "Don't get hung up on style." Frankly I think he was wrong. The way an individual behaves in negotiation is bound to have an impact on the people with whom he or she negotiates. But even if someone says or does something I find distasteful or offensive, I still have to determine whether he or she can help serve my interests. You have to ask yourself whether getting hung up on style is as important as reaching a conclusion that you find favorable.

## Negotiators' Sources of Power

### From: Alejandro, Mexico City, Mexico

**Question:** *I'm an MBA student and have a question about the sources of power that a negotiator can use during negotiation. I know a negotiator can have a certain power when he uses the right information and prepares for his negotiation, and/or when he uses his position (political or organizational) as leverage. Are there any more?*

**Response:** 1. The fundamental source of a negotiator's power is his/her knowledge of what resources s/he controls that can be used to solve the problem under consideration. If you have all the resources you need to take care of the issue, to meet your objectives, you have a great deal of power and may not need to negotiate with anyone to achieve those objectives. For example, many companies have the capacity to continue using their own facilities, staff, or vending machines to provide coffee or snacks to their employees. Thus, when they enter negotiations with a catering company in order to outsource the drink and snack function for their employees, the company has a very strong BATNA (Best Alternative to a Negotiated Agreement). Unless the caterer can provide service of equal or better quality for a lower price, the company has no reason to change its approach.

2. In your list of sources of power, you include a negotiator's position in the organizational hierarchy. It is important to remember that you may be in a position that empowers you to give orders; unless the people who are subordinate to you take you and your orders seriously, their performance may not reach the goals you have set. So, a hard-nosed boss may be "in charge" but may not be a sufficiently credible leader to inspire her subordinates to follow directions.

3. As crucial as it is to understand your own resources, your own BATNA, it is at least as important to understand the resources and BATNA of the parties with whom you are negotiating. Often people assume they have less power than other parties. You need to ask questions and listen very closely to the answers to find out whether that assumption is correct.

4. It follows from item 3 that one of the most significant sources of power in negotiation is based on one's capacity to listen and gain information. Information is the fundamental asset in negotiation. You do not learn by listening to yourself. There's an old expression: "God gave us two ears and one mouth. We should use them in that ratio."

---

## Stories, Parables, and Humor

### From: Eyal, Haifa, Israel

**Question:** *I have found that many people use stories to break the "flow" of a negotiation. Sometimes this makes the other side more nervous, even though the stories are related to the subject and to the situation. Would you please advise on possible sources for such stories, which may be sorted by subject and situation.*

**Response:** Because information is the fundamental asset of negotiation, sometimes a story presents a parable that can help illustrate a point. The most useful stories are real ones from your own experience or from the experience of people you know. Sometimes a joke works just as well—to make a point, to give people time to think about what is really going on, to give the other side a chance to see a different perspective on the issue. It all depends on your objectives.

If you are looking for sources of stories, there are certainly dozens of books—generally books of humor—that contain gems of wisdom. Having a sense of humor can help you find the entertaining elements of virtually any situation.

---

# Brainstorming, Inventing Options, and Creativity

### From: Miri, Penang, Malaysia

**Question:** *First, what is the difference, if any, between brainstorming and inventing options in the negotiation arena? Having read various versions this is a little confusing. Second, is it true that inventing options comes after the brainstorming process? In other words, you invent options for each action item based on the outcome of the brainstorm?*

**Response:** Sometimes you can view brainstorming and inventing options as isotopes of each other. It may make the most sense to say the two approaches can be grouped under the conceptual umbrella of creativity. What you learn from brainstorming gives you the opportunity to be more creative, to invent more options.

Brainstorming serves a very distinct additional function, as well: In negotiating, it is important to separate the people from the problem. Brainstorming normally does not involve saying, "This is Bill's idea, that is Charlie's idea, and that idea over there came from Eloise." Rather, each idea stands by itself and may lead to others, but is not burdened with "belonging" to any particular party.

In the first round of brainstorming, no idea is rejected. Once everything is written on the board or flipcharts, it is possible to winnow out suggestions that won't work and invent potentially workable options. This makes it somewhat easier to build consensus without saying, "If we adopt Bill's idea, then he wins."

---

## How Can I Be More Creative Under Pressure?

### From: Stephen, Lancashire, England

**Question:** *Sometimes when I am in a tough negotiation I find it difficult to be creative, and I worry that this weakness lets me down. I have been in sales for eight years; I've read many books and articles and have just finished a course on negotiation, but I have not found any information on this subject.*

**Response:** It is not realistic to think that you can look in the mirror and simply order yourself to "be creative." Creativity is often the result of the very uncreative activity of doing a good job of preparation. So, before you enter into a negotiation, it's a good idea to think hard about your interests and objectives, the interests and objectives of the person you'll be dealing with, and the interests and objectives of the constituencies or stakeholders of the parties who stand to gain or lose by the outcome of the negotiation.

Write out a diagram showing all the parties and stakeholders, possibly using arrows or lines to show connections among them. Some of those connections may include several of the parties or other stakeholders. Next, write down a series of assumptions about the interests and objectives of each stakeholder on the diagram. Each assumption ought to be tested before the formal negotiation process. It can help to have individual conversations with stakeholders who are not the primary negotiators. In addition, during the actual negotiation, asking questions to check the reality of each assumption can help you figure out what possible options exist for reaching agreement.

Your assumptions can also get your creative juices running, which will increase the likelihood that you will propose creative solutions to issues relevant to the negotiation.

## Split-Personality Negotiators

### From: Taha, Karachi, Pakistan

**Question:** *Should a good negotiator have more than one "personality"?*

**Response:** Good negotiators should not make a conscious choice to change their personality to fool other parties. A good negotiator has integrity, which is often more elaborately described as WYSIWYG (what you see is what you get). Generally speaking, people are uncomfortable negotiating with someone who has a hidden agenda. If the person I am negotiating with is hiding something from me, I will have difficulty trusting him. If I cannot trust him, then I cannot trust that he will fulfill the agreement we reach.

It is crucial to act with the understanding that negotiation is not a competitive sport. You compete with opponents, but you collaborate with people with whom you want to arrive at a durable, wise, and mutually satisfying agreement. A skilled negotiator needs to be able to comprehend the varied interests of the broadest possible range of stakeholders in any deal. The better one understands the interests of one's negotiation partner, the greater the likelihood that the negotiators will be able to reach an agreement each will willingly fulfill. That is the test of whether a negotiation has been successful.

Therefore, a good negotiator should not try to give the appearance of someone with multiple personalities, but rather someone with a well-integrated sense of herself that enables her to empathize with other stakeholders and find creative ways to bring the parties together in agreement.

## What's It All About?

### From: Wollie, Capetown, South Africa

**Question:** *Is negotiation all about achieving the best outcome for yourself (or your company), or is there more to it than that?*

**Response:** In one sense, negotiation is indeed all about achieving the best outcome. However—and this is critical—reaching a one-sided result is definitely not "achieving the best outcome."

When people negotiate for themselves, their companies, or other groups they represent, unless they reach an agreement to which both they and the other negotiating party or parties are committed, the negotiation is a failure. Virtually every negotiation should be viewed as an episode in an ongoing relationship, whether it is business or personal.

Thus a negotiator should aim at achieving the best for the parties involved in the negotiation as well as their constituencies. If only one party gains and others feel they have lost, the deal may fail to be fulfilled by the disappointed parties. Moreover, if the negotiation process leaves one or more parties grumbling, your reputation for fairness may suffer and folks will not want to do business with you in the future.

Achieving the best is a good goal if it is not one-sided. Achieving a wise resolution or agreement is probably a more accurate statement of the goal of good negotiation. If the result does not serve your company's interests, unless you have an awfully good reason for being disloyal, it does not serve your personal interests either.

---

# The Strengths and Weaknesses of a Good Negotiator

### From: Lolade, Lagos, Nigeria

**Question:** *What abilities will I be expected to have as a negotiator? I need to know this so that I will be able to identify my strengths and weaknesses.*

**Response:** Rather than giving you a long and detailed answer to your short question, here is a short list of several abilities one tends to find in good negotiators. You can figure out which of these qualities apply to you. A good negotiator generally:

- Comprehends who the stakeholders are in a negotiation and what their interests are.
- Asks good questions that yield useful information and convey a respect for other negotiators.

- Understands that negotiation is not a competitive sport.
- Is able to distinguish between interests and positions.
- Knows when to keep his mouth shut and his ears open.
- Recognizes that a negotiation is only successful if the parties reach an agreement each will willingly fulfill.
- Controls her emotions rather than letting her emotions control her.
- Prepares his strategy so he's not flying by the seat of his pants.
- Doesn't say anything that is contrary to her interest.
- Remembers that fast answers can lead to long consequences.
- Has the capacity to understand his own priorities—and the open-mindedness to accept that the priorities of others may be equally crucial to them.
- Realizes that each negotiation is different, but that the overall process is the same: using collaborative techniques to reach wise agreements.
- Uses empathy to try to understand the other party's points and objectives.
- Can tell the difference between interests and positions, and move people from positional bargaining to interest-based negotiation processes.

---

# Do Good Negotiation Skills Come From Nature or Nurture?

## From: Steve, Mill Valley, California

**Question:** *I am a 60-year-old self-employed environmental consultant. My 28-year-old son is making his living as a sports card trader, selling at conventions and online. He feels he is often out-negotiated by more seasoned hagglers—not necessarily card experts, but "bargaining" experts. He believes, I think incorrectly, that people with family-bred or business-trained bargaining skills have an insurmountable advantage.*

*I am writing to you because of my belief in the power of education, training, and guided practice. My wife is from Brooklyn, sells real estate for a living, and bargains for sport with folk-art sellers in every country she visits. She says bargaining is "in her blood." Even so, I want to believe my son and I can both learn to be better salesmen/negotiators in our respective fields. Which of our interpretations is correct?*

**Response:** You are all correct, to a point. Some people appear to be natural negotiators; just try reasoning with a four-year-old child. Every culture has its beliefs about what sorts of people make the best negotiators. Horse traders, New Englanders, and children are just some of the groups that are considered natural-born negotiators in American society. But for every skillful person in these and other groups, there are untold numbers of peers who can't negotiate their way out of a paper bag. It is difficult to imagine there's a gene for good negotiating!

The ability to negotiate is most often learned in one's home environment. One could say the same thing about one's taste in food, aesthetic leanings, and preferences for reading materials. Nurture is the major source of our negotiation style, enthusiasm about the process, and our skill (or lack thereof). If our family has not nurtured strong negotiation skills, it is possible to learn from experience on the job, by watching others, or from the influence of a mentor.

Formal negotiation training is a way to level the playing field. People who start off with good skills can enhance their ability through formal study. People who start off less sophisticated, less confident, or less competent can bring themselves up to speed if they participate in good seminars, read illustrative books, and take advantage of every opportunity to analyze and learn from every negotiation lesson they're offered.

Negotiation is not rocket science. It requires common sense and the capacity to think analytically, both prior to the negotiation and during the process. Your wife probably learned how to negotiate by being exposed to good negotiators in her family and in art markets all over the world. You and your son each have your own negotiation style and skills. Strengthening them through formal learning is readily accomplished, and can actually move you past those whose skills were developed through less formal means.

## Is Economics Everything?

### From: Nicolas, Angers, France

**Question:** *Why are economic factors so important when you negotiate?*

**Response:** People tend to want to keep score. This certainly holds true in negotiating. Normally negotiations are not accompanied by a referee or umpire who awards each negotiator points for creativity, good planning, or other impressive maneuvers. As a consequence, negotiators tend to look at the financial outcomes of their negotiation activities as the "score" by which their success or failure is measured.

Some negotiations really are just about money: "How much will the souvenir shop reduce its price for me?" "How little will this new employee accept as a starting salary?" While it's true that the majority of negotiations involve a financial element, the decision-making process in which the negotiating parties share must also take into account other issues, such as:

- How quickly can the product be delivered?
- Will the service yield the results you need?
- What impact might the result have on your ego?

As you can see, non-financial implications can be far more important than the financial ones.

The simple answer to your question is that economic factors can be important to people who are keeping score as they compete with other negotiators, but if the numbers are the only factors considered, there are strong odds the negotiators are going to miss more important issues.

## What's the Best Way to Ask Questions During a Negotiation?

### From: Amal, Jeddah, Saudi Arabia

**Question:** *I am a registered nurse. I have a lecture to give on negotiation and I was interested to learn that questioning is one of the most important tools* *one can use in negotiation. Can you kindly give me some information about questioning?*

**Response:** Information is the fundamental asset in negotiation. When we negotiate, I learn what you can offer me and you learn what I can offer you. We also learn what others find troublesome, boring, or irrelevant to their decision-making. The best way to gain information is to ask questions. Although there is no such thing as a dumb question, there can be unwise answers.

Figuring out what information a negotiator needs to obtain to reach wise conclusions is a crucial part of preparing for the negotiation process. Consider what you know about the person or people you'll be negotiating with, their constituents (the people who are depending on the results they achieve), and other stakeholders. Of course you should also consider your own constituents and stakeholders upon whom your actions may have an impact. By giving thought to all these issues, you will discover what information you need to gain and, therefore, what questions you need to ask.

There is another reason that good questioning is a crucial element of wise negotiation: asking people questions is a sign of respect. You are demonstrating you are interested in what the other party has to say, that you take them seriously. People who think they need to enter into a negotiation with guns blazing miss the point. Parties negotiate with one another because they have reason to believe/hope that collaboration will yield mutual gains. Attacking your counterpart's ideas may be construed as an attack on his or her ego.

Thus, asking questions is a crucial mechanism for establishing mutual respect and an atmosphere that can lead to cooperation in resolving problems.

---

## How to Be a Cool Negotiator

### From: Charlie, Norwalk, Connecticut

**Question:** *I'm 13 and need an answer. I heard that the basic things you need to do to be a good negotiator are: 1) act cool, 2) don't attract attention, and 3) never tell them the bad part of the deal. Is this true?*

**Response:** Acting cool is a good part of successful negotiation, but only if it is not just an act. The "coolness" you need for successful negotiation really means keeping a cool, analytical head. You should always prepare ahead of time and ask yourself: *What do I want and why do I want it? What do they want and why do they want it?* During the actual negotiation, you should find ways to take a step back from the discussion and look at what is going on with that same cool head: *Why did he/she say that? What arguments or tactics are being used that are convincing—or are turn-offs?*

The other side of the coin is that successful negotiators should be passionate about the interests they're pursuing. If you are passionately committed to something and you make that clear to others by expressing emotion, that can be far more convincing than keeping a "cool" demeanor.

Avoiding attracting attention is a bit of a problem in negotiation. People don't want to negotiate with someone who can't make and deliver on an agreement. You may not want outsiders to witness a negotiation, particularly if it involves a confidential issue. But to negotiate in the real world, you must be "all in" if you expect other parties to take your involvement in the process seriously.

If you negotiate without telling people about the bad part of the deal, they have every right to come back after the agreement and demand, "Why didn't you tell me about that?" Of course, you have to be sensible about how and when you communicate the bad news. Listen for questions that show you what others are likely to be worried about. If they ask a direct question, tell the truth. If they aren't direct with their questions, but you know the issue would be important to you if you were in their shoes, there's nothing wrong with trying to find out if they care about that issue as much as you do. Your parents may disapprove of a particular song or group; another person may not have that problem. So what's bad news for you may not be bad news for them.

Don't forget, you can fight fires without burning bridges.

# Controlling Anger for Effective Negotiating

## From: Pat, Canton, Massachusetts

**Question:** *How can people control their anger so they can be more effective negotiators?*

**Response:** An old friend told me of an interesting rule at his family's dinner table: "Only one person is allowed to be angry at a time." There are often excellent reasons for getting angry or upset: parties may offer outrageous proposals, they may launch personal attacks, or they may feel victimized or otherwise aggrieved. Not letting others know that something is very important to you hurts you in the sense that you are bottling up your emotions—and it hurts them because they may not achieve the level of understanding of the issues that can assist in crafting a solution.

A few more rules about anger:

- If you don't let it all hang out, you may be withholding useful information.
- Taking things personally may blind you to their interests, the building blocks that can lead to resolution.
- If more than one party escalates the emotional level of the discussion, it leads to greater heat, but not greater light.

When you are tempted to get angry, remember to check whether or not it is your turn. If it is someone else's turn to get angry, sit there and take it—and reward yourself by reminding yourself how wonderful you are to be in such control of your emotions. When people vent their emotions, ultimately they will reach an end point. Their heart rate slows, their breathing becomes calmer, and they are far more likely to be amenable to more "civilized" approaches to problem-solving.

Remember to ask yourself whether the problem would disappear if a particular person were to disappear. More often than not, the person is not the problem; the problem is the problem. That perspective can also help keep things from escalating.

Don't try to resolve issues by acting out the negotiation equivalent of road rage; innocent people can get caught in the crossfire. Wisely expressed emotions can be used to underscore the importance of an issue, so don't be afraid to express your feelings. Just make sure you do it in a strategically wise fashion.

---

# Effective Agreements

### From: Mimi, Alberta, Canada

**Question:** *What are the characteristics of an effective "competitive" bargainer? What are some other forms of alternative dispute resolution? Also, please tell me some key features of an effective agreement and how to get one.*

**Response:** Your questions go to the heart of the various negotiating styles and how to choose one. Competitive bargaining has also been described as distributive, adjudicative, or zero-sum bargaining. In competitive bargaining, you have a winner and a loser. Very rarely do both or all parties in a competitive negotiation walk away feeling equally pleased with the results. A competitive bargainer takes the approach that this negotiation is a one-shot deal: *Whatever I can "win" now is all I care about. My future relationship with the person with whom I am negotiating is either of no consequence to me or is based on their understanding that whenever they negotiate with me, I am going to come out on top.*

Competitive strategies can succeed in the short term. In the long term, however, most people will go out of their way to avoid negotiating with a competitive bargainer. In your personal life, if people figure out that negotiating with you is a losing proposition, they may tend to avoid you. In business, it is equally dire: If potential customers or suppliers assume that you'll steamroll over them, they are likely to look for alternative people or companies to do business with. The result of the competitive approach often means that the other party leaves the negotiation grumbling, "If that so-and-so thinks I'm going to live up to that bargain he rammed down my throat, he'll have to take me to court!"

Never forget: negotiation is not a competitive sport.

Interest-based negotiation is a far more realistic approach for reaching wise, fair, durable agreements using efficient, respectful, mutually rewarding processes. Skillful interest-based negotiators are also more likely to enhance relationships that are beneficial in both business and personal situations. The process is a fair one, and both parties are able to find areas of mutual agreement upon which to build a resolution. This is because the negotiators are considering not only their own immediate personal interests, but also the consequences for other parties of any agreement they reach. Successful negotiation is a process that leads to an agreement each party will willingly fulfill.

An effective agreement addresses the interests of all parties, keeping in mind such issues as fairness, the relationship, the capacity and willingness of each party to make a commitment and implement it, and the creativity each party employs to add value to the process and the agreement itself.

---

## Critiques of Principled Negotiation Needed

### From: Ben, Queensland, Australia

**Question:** *I'm currently doing a paper for my MBA on principled negotiation. I'm finding it hard to find any literature that is critical of the principled negotiation approach. Could you describe for me specific types of conflicts or negotiations where the principled negotiation approach may not be advisable?*

**Response:** Principled negotiation, more properly called "interest-based negotiation," is by far the best way for parties to resolve virtually all disputes. Even in the case of the seemingly interminable "Troubles" in Northern Ireland, interest-based negotiation was able to bring about the Good Friday Agreement, which appears to have achieved what political wrangling, incivility, and outright warfare could not.

I am not familiar with a body of literature that takes a negative view of interest-based negotiation. While there remain some commercial teachers of negotiation techniques who appear to encourage the use of "slash and burn" approaches, when one examines the syllabi of their courses, one finds that they, too, encourage course members to aim for a win/win resolution. Most assuredly, one can find articles and books that tweak interest-based techniques to make them more effective. There are also published books that describe "dirty" negotiation tactics; the ones that I have examined explain how to counter such tactics, for the most part using interest-based strategies and techniques.

The important thing to understand in viewing interest-based negotiation is that it is not organized like a pre-flight checklist where one must choose a particular route in every situation. Rather, interest-based techniques offer a variety of choices the negotiator can make based on the understanding that every situation is different.

## Why Positional Bargaining Is Dumb

### From: Ronnie, Pretoria, South Africa

**Question:** *I read that "position-based bargaining is inefficient, endangers ongoing relations and becomes increasingly ineffective." What are your thoughts on this?*

**Response:** Here are some thoughts you might be able to use: The positional approach to negotiation, in which the process is viewed as a zero-sum game, does greater damage to the positional bargainer than other parties. A positional bargainer has locked herself into position; moving out of that position will most likely yield a loss of face. Even worse, moving away from a position may well diminish the credibility of the positional bargainer so substantially that her reputation suffers.

By taking this approach, positional bargainers are making it clear that they do not intend to play fair in their negotiations with others. People on the receiving end of this treatment are going to be reluctant to enter into an agreement. If they feel coerced into one, they will be on the lookout for any opportunity to breach it. Because successful negotiation is a process by which people reach agreements that each party is ready, willing, and able to fulfill, when an unfair process yields an agreement that a party is neither ready, willing, nor able to fulfill, that is a failed negotiation.

The long-term consequences of using a positional approach include greater difficulty in finding people willing to negotiate with you, a reputation for narrowness and closed-mindedness, and great difficulty establishing and maintaining the reciprocity necessary in rewarding human relationships.

## Struggling With the Basics

### From: Synala, New Zealand

**Question:** *Why, when we are looking at the same thing, do we have differing perceptions? What are some possible drawbacks to this during negotiations?*

**Response:** Having different perceptions of the same object is a fundamental human characteristic. Whether we differ about the glass being half empty or half full, or whether witnesses to an automobile accident come up with conflicting descriptions of the circumstances, all we are doing is behaving normally. While it may be a frustrating fact of life, it is almost impossible to conceive of a single absolute truth upon which everyone can agree.

For example, I do not think that focusing on the disadvantages of differing perceptions is the right approach. Instead, we should focus on the potential benefits. If your interests are complementary to mine, that means we both stand a chance of having our interests served—and we don't have to go to war because we are fighting over the same thing.

If everyone were the same, life would be terribly boring. Valuing differences can make us all richer and more fulfilled.

## Measuring the Qualities of a Good Negotiator

### From: Mridula, Kochi, India

**Question:** *All educational interventions aim at enhancing the life skills of young people. However, we know that training and educational interventions focus on imparting information that may increase the knowledge and understanding related to specific content, but do not build the skills—especially negotiation skills—necessary for facing the challenges of life. I am working in the area of adolescent reproductive health and am developing indicators that can help teachers/workers plan their interventions and assess their impact in terms of enhancing life skills among young people.*

*I am looking at negotiation skills as an outcome of thinking and social skills. Thinking skills include self-awareness and social awareness, decision-making, problem-solving, and goal-setting. Social skills include establishing relationships and listening and communicating effectively. Negotiation skills are a result of rational thinking based on informed choices and effective communication to get one's ideas/plans accepted by the other person. Thus, to negotiate rationally and effectively, one needs to enhance thinking and social skills. It is a process of self-realization and development that is facilitated by others who are mature and thinking individuals. Adolescents and young people need to know how to negotiate with others for a healthy and happy life and to overcome the strong influence of peer pressure for experimenting with drugs, alcohol, and sex.*

*Literature related to negotiation skills refers to negotiation as an activity that is done with another person. The need for negotiation with self is not understood. In our experience of the life skills training in this area of India, we have realized that negotiating with self is a prerequisite for negotiating with others. What do we understand by negotiating with self? It means making decisions regarding the people/activities to get involved with, the extent of involvement, and when and how to detach or wean off. Attachment or involvement is necessary for quality, and detachment is essential for sustainability. Being involved yet aloof, or detached, requires reflection, vision, and spirituality. Living in the present, not brooding on the past, and working toward the future, requires negotiating with self.*

*Can you offer any suggestions/references for developing indicators for negotiation skills? Thanks.*

**Response:** Thank you for your very insightful comments about negotiation and its relationship to rational thinking and interpersonal decision-making. You have made me think and reflect in some new directions and I am indebted to you for that. At the end of your note you asked for indicators for assessing the negotiation skills of people. For me, the first point of investigation is to determine what constitutes a successful negotiation. Successful negotiation is a process by which two or more people reach an agreement which each is committed to fulfill. If we use that as our point of departure, I find it difficult to arrive at indicia or benchmarks to assess the skills of an individual negotiator. However here are some elements to consider. A good negotiator:

- Understands her interests and those of others.
- Understands the BATNA (Best Alternative to a Negotiated Agreement) available to herself and others.

- Knows how important the relationship with the other party is.
- Uses creativity in order to expand the possibilities to bring about agreement.
- Remembers that fairness in the negotiation process increases the likelihood of agreement.
- Understands the capacity and willingness of each party to make and fulfill a commitment.
- Ensures a free exchange of information, the fundamental asset in every negotiation.

Each negotiation is unique. Perhaps one can measure the capacity of a negotiator to listen and communicate, but I find it difficult to think of objective measures for determining the capacity of a person to comprehend his/her own interests, much less those of others. For example, several years ago I needed a new car. My back had been bothering me, so what sold me on the car I purchased was the quality of its seat and its capacity to provide me good support. I was very focused on my interest in taking care of my back. On the other hand, being so focused on my back, I did a lousy job of focusing on my financial interest; my desire for the car was so obvious that the salesman was able to get a much higher price from me than if I had been paying closer attention to my financial interest instead of my body's interest. In other words, except in extraordinarily simple negotiation situations, things are too complex to assess the talents of any one party via dry, objective criteria.

An airplane pilot must go through a comprehensive checklist before starting a flight, and the right answers are always the same. In negotiation, there is no pre-defined checklist. To be a good negotiator, one must be able to talk slowly and think fast. One must be flexible and imaginative. One must have a clear enough sense of one's interests to be prepared to walk away if necessary—or to hang in there and keep trying to make a deal, no matter how tough the other side may be.

The indicators for assessing negotiation skills change with each set of circumstances. They are different for people as they pass through different ages, or find themselves in different situations. Negotiations with a spouse are different than negotiations with one's children or one's parents. No single skill set works every time; you need to have an understanding of the choices available to you—and hopefully make the right choice more often than you make the wrong choice from a procedural standpoint.

# Chapter 2

# All in the Family

---

## Her Lying Drives Me Crazy

### From: Shabana, Mumbai, India

**Question:** *The issue is that I live with my mother-in-law. My husband and I do not have enough money to buy a house of our own. We also have a 2-year-old baby who needs care while we are at work. My mother-in-law helps take care of our baby. Unfortunately I always end up having serious arguments with her every few days. The thing is that some things about her personality tick me off. One of her vices is lying needlessly and deliberately. I feel we would be so much better off if she just dealt with issues honestly, but she seems unable to stop the lying. This hurts me and makes me really angry. I would love to deal directly and straightforwardly with her. I find it insulting when people lie to me, but she does not seem willing or able to give up this habit.*

*I have never violated her trust in any way for her to behave like this toward me. The fact is, she never placed any trust in me from the beginning, and still treats me as an outsider. I have been living with her for three years now. How do I deal with this and negotiate a solution we can all be happy with?*

37

**Response:** I share your distaste for people who lie. If your circumstances mean that you must continue to share housing with your mother-in-law for a long time, it is you who must make the adjustment; she is not going to change. It would be wise to think of how you can change your situation: are there other relatives with whom you could live? Can you and your husband develop a five-year plan (for example) to secure different housing?

Does your husband share your sensitivity to his mother's lies? If you're unsure, don't say to him, "Your mother is a no-good liar!" Rather, when she lies in your husband's presence, "question" him with your eyes; see whether he notices and how he reacts.

One thing you can do is decide that it is her job in life to lie. Try to count how many times a day she lies; see if she can set a record. Since you know that is her nature, you should figure that unless she lies, she is failing to live up (or down) to your expectations of her. When she lies, say to yourself, "There she goes again!" Make it a game, knowing that you win by being amused, that since you expect her to disappoint you, every time she does so, you win.

---

## Whose Money Is It Anyway?

### From: Joan, Armonk, New York

**Question:** *Before my father died (more than 10 years ago), my older sister had asked him for a $27,000 advance on her share of the inheritance for a house down payment. He agreed, and according to my sister, they each signed a paper stating that when the inheritance was to be awarded to her, that $27,000 would be withheld, as that amount had already been given to her.*

*After my father's death, when the court date came around (it took place in Munich, Germany, where he had lived), this signed paper, which my father's widow would have possessed, could not be found; therefore, the court awarded my sister her entire inheritance, including the previously advanced $27,000. This meant that his widow and his four other children did not receive our share of $27,000.*

*On the court date, his widow decided to give up her share of the $27,000 (her share being 50 percent of that, or $13,500) in order not to have to postpone* *the court proceedings. His widow said that the siblings could have her share and divide it amongst themselves. The result of all of this was that my sister decided to keep the extra $27,000 that the court had awarded her. My brother and I tried to talk to her about the fact that although the court had awarded her this money, from an ethical point of view, it actually was not hers to keep. She responded by calling us "moneygrubbers," and claimed that the initial $27,000 had been not an advance but a gift from our father to her, and that she had never asked our father for anything, whereas he had paid for my college tuition (which incidentally was very low) and for a car for our brother.*

*We have not been in contact with one another since then, except for a few civil phone calls to see how the other is doing. Now, my sister's daughter has asked me to attend her wedding this June. I would like to attend to support my niece, and I am undecided as to how to approach my sister, as it will be the first time in years that we will have seen one another. I am inclined not to mention the issue, as it is my niece's wedding day; however, my sister will probably invite me to stay with her, which I am not sure I feel comfortable doing. She is willing to act as if nothing ever happened, but I am uncomfortable doing the same, because I feel that her actions were unjust and hurtful to myself as well as my siblings. I would like to resolve this difficult situation, but I do not know how to begin. Incidentally, she lives in California and I live in New York.*

**Response:** The question you ask really raises two very separate issues. The first is whether you attend your niece's wedding. Unless you are a believer in the philosophy that children should be punished for the sins of their parents, if you want to maintain or improve your relationship with your niece, you should attend the wedding and give the bride and groom an appropriate gift that bears no reflection on your troubles with her mother.

The second issue involves dealing with something that still makes your blood boil after more than a decade. You need to give close consideration to your priorities: do you have an interest in reestablishing a civil and perhaps even closer relationship with your sister? Does her ethical failure trouble you more because it appears she has been dishonest, because you need the money, or because she has treated you and the other members of the family with disrespect? If your share of the $27,000 represents a very significant part of the inheritance and you need the money, perhaps that should be the governing factor. Unfortunately, unless documentary proof can be found that the cash was an advance on the inheritance, I doubt you will have much success using lawyers or other professionals.

If your sister invites you to be a guest in her house, there is nothing wrong in telling her you are uncomfortable being under the same roof with someone who you feel treated you and other members of the family unfairly. However, this will raise the old argument(s) and not resolve the inheritance issue. It may satisfy your sense of justice, but unless you find a new approach to take, it is not likely to change the facts that have persisted since your father's death.

You could respond to your sister's invitation of hospitality by saying, "There remains in my gut a feeling of injustice in terms of the way you dealt with your share of the inheritance. Do you think we could find some way to heal our relationship in a way that leaves us both more comfortable?" Just giving her a yes-or-no choice, such as, "I'll stay at your house if you send me a check for my share," will not necessarily give her a chance to make a more creative choice. For example, she may not want to give you any money, but there may be a piece of art, an old book, or some other item she has from your father that could be a symbolic thing she could give you to increase your share of the inheritance. Perhaps there is an old family bible, a valuable family heirloom, or something else your father had which could be given to you as a gesture of reconciliation.

Making the whole issue revolve around money puts both of you in hard positions; neither of you can give in without losing face. Letting her know your feelings are hurt and that your top priority is to get on with a more positive relationship can open the door. Even if your sister doesn't invite you to stay in her home, you can let her know that you are going to the wedding for your niece. Perhaps your sister will offer to pay for a nice hotel room or pay for your airfare. Look for symbols that will respond to your interests.

Your interests may be short- or long-term, but unless you know why a particular resolution will make you feel better, the resolution might not give you the long-term ease of heart you need.

## It's My Inheritance; Do I Have to Share It?

### From: Milton, San Bernardino, California

**Question:** *Soon I will inherit $100,000 or so. I plan on putting it in my own personal bank account. Will I have to share it with my wife? She never liked my mom. How should I deal with this?*

**Response:** These sorts of questions can be addressed two ways. You can make a unilateral decision, but should get the advice of a lawyer to make sure you are obeying the law. While you may get the money now, if your denial of a share of the money to your wife sours your relationship with her, the funds may be counted as assets in a divorce—even after you have spent the money.

Thus, looking at this second factor is really the one that counts. In negotiation you have to consider many factors: interests, BATNA (Best Alternative to a Negotiated Agreement), communication, and others. One of those "others" is relationship. Before deciding to keep the money for yourself and away from your wife, you should consider how that decision could affect your marital relationship. Your wife may well have never liked your mom, but the far more important question is whether you and she like/love each other and whether money is worth jeopardizing that relationship.

## They Treated Us Like Dirt, but We Want to Do the Right Thing

### From: Laura, Rogers, Arkansas

**Question:** *My problem is with my mother-in-law. Things have been difficult from the very beginning. Three months after we began dating, his mother called my husband crying and told him that he needed to come over. My husband thought that she must need to discuss some health problems and worried all night until he was able to see her. We even cancelled an appointment with a realtor to look at a house in order for him to go and talk with her. It ended up that she just wanted to tell him that she felt like she was losing her son (even though he was still officially living in her house at that time). She* *cried and became all emotional. That was just the beginning of our problems with the in-laws.*

*After that it seemed that every couple of months, his mother would throw a fit, and it always seemed to coincide with a major stepping-stone in our relationship: buying a house, holidays, getting engaged, wedding planning. Every time his mother would throw a fit and create a problem from nothing, his parents would expect us to come over and talk about it. My husband would explain to them that there was nothing to talk about because the problem was either her twisting the truth or simply creating something out of nothing. Our feeling was that we shouldn't give her the attention that she wanted, just for throwing a fit. However, throughout this time I continued to encourage my husband to call his parents, stop by for a visit, and invite them over, which they declined four out of the six times we invited them.*

*The final straw was when we joined them for a trip to Disney World. We stayed together, but we paid our own way. On the last night, which was my husband's birthday and two months before our wedding, my mother-in-law threw another fit. She called me every name in the book, from "that thing" to "bit%$." Her fit this time was because we walked too fast through the theme parks and I was "trying to lose her." At no time throughout the week did she say that we were going too fast, or that she needed to stop and rest. Throughout the entire slinging of mud and evil words, I was very proud of my husband and myself and how we handled ourselves. At no time did we call names, insult her, or raise our voice in a harsh tone. She was the only one who used foul names and said that she wouldn't have anything to do with me any longer. She even said that my husband was welcome at their home, but I was no longer a part of their lives. At one point in the evening she wrote a short note to my husband and stated that she wished that someone would just shoot both her and her husband. My husband and I were shocked that she would put him in such a terrible spot. Of course my husband said that if I wasn't invited around them, he wasn't either, and that she needed some professional help.*

*My husband ended up e-mailing them and explained that he wanted to fix things, but that we needed a sincere apology before we could move on. His mother wrote us back a letter with both of their names signed at the bottom. The letter was 100 times worse and more hateful than what she had said in Orlando. She insulted my family, called my 5-year-old son a manipulative brat, and again verbally assaulted my character and made up lies about me that my husband knew were not true. She told my husband that he was blinded by my brainwashing and that even his grandmother, grandfather, uncle and his wife all can see how horrible I am. But when we asked each of them, they were shocked that she said those horrible things and apologized again and again. We ended up getting married two and a half months after her last fit, and his parents refused to come to the wedding. She has continued to badmouth me to other people in my husband's family.*

*The problem now is that I am pregnant. I will have the baby in three months. When we found out that we were expecting, I urged my husband to call his parents because I didn't feel that it would be right for his parents to find out through the grapevine. They were so excited, but refused to offer any apology for the torment that they had put us through. The closest thing to an apology was his father admitting that things had been said out of anger. I disagree with this. I felt that it was an attempt to break us up before the wedding.*

*I'm not sure what to do because they are acting with my husband as though there was no longer a problem, and that things will just blow over. I haven't received an apology yet but even if I do, I honestly am not sure if I will be able to face her. Should I stay firm on expecting a sincere apology even though now she's trying to say that she was never mad at me, but more at my husband for letting it get to the point that it did? How should I handle the birth of our baby and my husband's parents?*

**Response:** The first thing you need to do is a careful analysis of your interests, those of your husband, and those of your children. Interests are not your specific goals or objectives, but rather the reason those goals or objectives are important to you (or another party). You need to ask why each of the people on your "team" should want to improve the relationship with your in-laws. Take a look at such factors as ego, reputation, the example to be set for your children, and your husband's chance to benefit from a good long-term relationship with his parents. Think also of what might be thought of as negative interests: the risks of your children absorbing the apparently dishonest or dishonorable example set by the in-laws, the toll the stress of the situation brings on yourself and/or your relationship with your husband, and the impact on you and your husband of having to choose between family and self.

In other words, you need to approach the whole situation as rationally as possible. You need to analyze the likely consequences of any approach you might take on your short- and long-term well-being. Think about who all the stakeholders are, too. In addition to you and your husband and children, there may also be aunts, uncles, cousins, members of your family, friends and neighbors, or members of other groups with whom you identify. Think about your in-laws' stake in things—and the people (other than yourselves) who depend on them or take their well-being seriously.

If you prepare very thoughtfully and analytically, you are more likely to choose objectives, strategies, and tactics that make sense under the circumstances. Take the advice of trusted friends, clergy, or others who will not judge you or your in-laws but only comment on the situation. Find allies among the extended family—ask them for advice, and solicit their input on the possible approaches you might take. That makes them far more likely to buy into the resolution you reach and can help build favorable relationships that may be more rewarding.

In negotiation, the past has no future. That means that the reason to negotiate is not to change history or the interpretation of history. Rather, people negotiate to try to change the future. If you decide that finding a way to remedy the situation with your in-laws is important or serves your interests, you may have to bite the bullet and forget about apologies. Apologies are important in negotiation, but it could be better to say something such as, "We are very excited about our new child and hope she or he has the joy of knowing you as loving grandparents." You have to decide in advance whether you are prepared to make a concession regarding the apology, which certainly sounds much-needed. If the grandchildren's future is an issue about which you and your in-laws can agree, make that a building block for beginning to develop a healed relationship. Pain and dishonesty can linger a long time—forgiving can take place without forgetting.

In your planning, determine what your boundaries are in terms of the behavior of the grown-ups (you and your in-laws) with each other, with the children, and with friends and family. These lines ought to be discussed so that you reach agreement. If the lines are kept secret, no one can be blamed for accidentally crossing them.

You have to think and plan and develop a reasonably clear sense of what is acceptable in the immediate situation and over the long term. Be ready for changes, and know when to roll with the punches—and when not to.

# What a Fine Mess We've Gotten Into

## From: Tom, Dallas, Texas

**Question:** *My wife and I are newly married. From before that time, my now mother-in-law has been nothing but unpleasant toward us. She gives us a lot of gifts, but they are designed to "guilt" us into giving her affection, even though she treats us coldly.*

*I think this all started with a confrontation we had one night. It was about my sister-in-law's then boyfriend; he was kind of slimy, and I made it known in an inappropriate way. I apologized afterward and did the best I could to stomach him. She, however, was cold to me from then on. It escalated when the boyfriend dumped my sister-in-law and showed his true colors in action. I was happy it was over but kept it to myself. I started getting this resentment from my mother-in-law, I think, because I was right about him.*

*My wife and I became pregnant before we got married, but it would not have changed much because we were planning to elope. My mother-in-law, on the other hand, was planning a big "to-do" wedding. The wedding she put together was fine, but she guilt-tripped us the whole time, saying it so shameful and talking about our news as "the situation." She never seemed excited about their first grandchild.*

*Nowadays, the gifts of little meaning, just something to buy, keep coming. She won't get excited when we ask her to feel the baby kick; she only says she "had the same thing." When we declined her self-invitation to the sonogram (where we found out we were having a boy), she was hurt, and instead of being happy to be the first to know, after us, she shunned us. My wife was very hurt that no one called to find out or congratulate us. That was it for me. I had had enough of her childish treatment of us. Since then, nothing has gotten better. We stayed at their home last weekend, but we felt like we were burdens the entire time, even though we cleaned up after ourselves and cooked and ran errands for her.*

*I'm sorry this is so long but she has been emotionally abusing my wife to the point of eating disorders and antidepressants for years. I don't want my new baby to have this waiting for him, too.*

**Response:** The situation you describe is a very difficult one. You should probably get a very large piece of paper and fill it with all the stakeholders in this complex situation: yourself, your wife, your child, your sister-in-law, your mother-in-law, other friends and relations, and whoever else might be impacted by the complexities of the relationships. After you have listed the stakeholders, include what you assume to be their interests—for example, a congenial family relationship, healing existing damage, ego issues to overcome such as guilt and resentment, potential financial consequences, and the many other factors that the various people involved might find important.

Your next step should be to figure out what possible outcomes could lead to the satisfaction of those interests or the amelioration of the troubles you describe. Take special care to discuss the possibilities, and the assumed interests themselves, with those people with whom you enjoy an open and honest relationship that isn't fraught with emotional risks. Obviously you and your wife run major emotional risks in your own relationship, but hopefully you can deal with each other openly and collaboratively.

Your objective in all of this is to figure out how various stakeholders can reason together on a collaborative basis to resolve or improve your circumstances. Keep your eye on the options available to you. In negotiation language, that's called your BATNA, your Best Alternative to a Negotiated Agreement. In other words, when might it make sense to walk away and abandon the negotiation and choose an alternative way of solving the problem? What would happen to you, your wife, your son—and the other people involved—if you were to cut off your relationship with your mother-in-law? Consider your alternatives, and the short- and long-term consequences they might yield.

When you and your wife are on the same page about all these issues, you should be far more prepared to take the appropriate steps to improve your extended family relationship.

## Why Did He Blow Up About His Birthday?

### From: May, Ulm, Germany

**Question:** *My husband's birthday is coming up and I was planning on having a surprise birthday party for him. The problem is that he does not want anyone to be here in our home or have any parties at all. I have already planned* *everything and called all his friends. Now I have to call all of them and cancel it due to his screaming and freaking out about the party. He knows about the party because he forced me into telling him what my plans were; when I told him about it, he blew up, saying, "It's my birthday and I don't want anyone here!" I'm pretty sad about what he did and I need advice on how to negotiate this situation.*

**Response:** The situation you describe is not directly an issue of negotiation; you have already acquiesced to your husband's demands that the birthday party be cancelled.

The real question is what your objectives are in the future. You probably would be wise to try to learn why a birthday party—or particularly a surprise party—causes your husband to be so upset. It might be as simple—and loving—as only wanting to share his celebration with you. On the other hand, it could reflect some more serious issues, and because such issues might have an impact on your relationship, you certainly should try to find out what is going on.

Ask questions that are open-ended , which require more than a yes-or-no answer. Be careful to think about the best words to use in your questioning process as well as the optimal time to raise those questions. Be especially attentive to what your husband's answers tell you about himself—and you.

---

## Getting Through to My Husband

### From: Fanny, Odessa, Texas

**Question:** *Sometimes I feel like my husband's mother. Here's the situation: Two weeks before our marriage last year we received full custody of my husband's two children. We both work from 8 to 5, but I do most of the housework. He will help but only when I ask, and it's at his leisure. This irks me because the whole time he's cleaning he asks me where the sponges are, where's this and where's that, even though they've been in the same spot for four years.*

*I have learned to deal with this. What really bothers me is that he'll agree with me about something and then just turn around and do the complete opposite—maybe just to shut me up? For example, there is no smoking in our house, and he agrees with me about this. Last night his friend and wife came over, and my husband allowed them to smoke in the house. I asked him if they had been smoking and his reply was, "Maybe. I think so." I know he knew when they lit up; he just didn't care. I'm allergic to smoke and he is an asthmatic.*

*I feel like he's rebelling against me. Those are the vibes I get from him. Also, once a week he'll call me and tell me he wants to come home from work because he's having a bad day. I'm not his mom but I have to tell him, "No, you have to work—we have bills, and children." This results in him being mad at me, and the "rebelling " happens soon after that.*

*Help! I love him and want to work with him, but I don't know how to get him to hear me.*

**Response:** Despite what you say in your first sentence, it sounds as if you have accepted the job of "mothering" your husband. There are a number of steps you need to take. The first is to examine your interests in this situation. You can start by looking at your objectives, but then you have to dig down deeper to figure out why a particular objective is appropriate for you. For example, you want to ban smoking from your surroundings—that is your objective. The interests you want to serve by doing away with smoking in your vicinity may include protecting your health, possibly having a cleaner house, reducing dry-cleaning costs, and setting a good example for the children.

Once you have done a reasonably good job of figuring out what your interests are, then you should do the same thing in terms of your husband's interests. What does he want from you, and why does he want it? Then you have to figure out whether his objectives and interests are compatible with yours. If you find compatibility, that means you have a sense of how you can appeal to his interests and convince him to do things differently.

It sounds as if you should also do something else before undertaking any discussions with your husband; you should figure out your BATNA (Best Alternative to a Negotiated Agreement) and his BATNA, as well. If you don't negotiate with him, or if you begin negotiations and feel you're not getting anywhere, or if he agrees to something and then does the opposite, what can you do? Do you simply accept the situation? Do you walk away from the relationship? Do you have other tools you can use to improve the situation? Once you have a good understanding of your respective

BATNAs, the choices you can make, you will be better prepared to negotiate with him.

As things stand, it sounds as if he's getting everything he wants without fulfilling his responsibilities, as though he were an uncooperative child. Moreover, it sounds as if you are enabling this situation to continue. You should consider your options very seriously; do the rewards really outweigh the annoyances?

## My Wife Badmouths Me—and My Family

### From: Charles, Harare, Zimbabwe

**Question:** *I have been married for three years and have a two and a half-year-old son. My wife appears to be in love with me but does not respect what I say and doesn't seem to share the same vision with me for the family. She doesn't seem to like my relatives, which is demonstrated in the way she receives and treats them when they visit us. She always wants to find fault in whatever they do and then bring it to my attention. She wants me to act in a way that pleases her—something I find difficult to do after analyzing the situation and finding no wrongdoing on my part or that of my family. She has proven to be a difficult person to handle. I have tried to negotiate with her but she still says bad things about me to my own family. What should I do?*

**Response:** Your situation requires careful analysis. You must figure out what drives your decisions about what is right and wrong, about what you want for yourself, your son, your relatives—and your wife's family, as well. One step you can take is to draw an Interest Map, a chart that shows all the stakeholders and what their interests are, which will give you a sense of what you know for sure and what you need to find out to go forward properly prepared. Make sure you distinguish between facts and assumptions, and remember that what one person believes to be a fact can actually be a believed assumption. Check the reality of your assumptions and try to figure out what questions you need to ask your wife to learn more about what drives her thinking and decision-making.

Asking questions is a way of showing respect, and is far more likely to bring you information than relying on assumptions or even what you believe to be scientifically demonstrable facts. It is crucial, however, to ask only open-ended questions rather than ones that can be answered with a yes or no. It is also important to avoid asking questions that make you sound like a police interrogator. Asking someone to admit that they are bad pretty much guarantees they will get worse; it certainly offers them no incentive to change their behavior. Negotiation is about trading: "*If you will do X, then I will do Y.*" Don't be afraid of making concessions, but each concession must be tied to a reward for you.

Take a look at what choices you can make and what choices are open to your wife. Try to figure out the source of her unfriendly attitude, whether it is your behavior or habits, the challenges of life as a young parent, your economic circumstances, or something else. If the biggest problems are really not central to your relationship but rather are external, you and your wife could work to become a team to deal with whatever external issues are problems that you share.

Your problem will take great sensitivity and creativity to resolve, and only collaboration between you and your wife will yield a resolution that works. A successful negotiation is a process that leads to an agreement each party will willingly fulfill.

## Negotiating With a 15-Year-Old

### From: Albert, Marietta, Georgia

**Question:** *I feel like I am always being manipulated by my child, who is all of 15. What general or specific tips do you have for me?*

**Response:** It often appears that 15-year-olds are not only obligated, but *empowered* to manipulate their parents. When my two daughters were around that age, it was clear to me that daughters are especially powerful as father-controllers. My dogs try some of the same things, but are less powerful because they do not know how to prepare their own meals.

More seriously, you need to take a look at the issues that are on and off the table with a child. Children are often excellent negotiators because the process is more important to them than the results. Because results are merely the pretext for the negotiation process, they have less at stake in the outcome than parents who are stuck with a longer-term view of things. Thus, it makes sense to listen closely to what your child is saying and what he is not saying. Figuring out how those two facets of the negotiation relate to each other will help you gain entry into the process.

Put yourself in his shoes. When we recognize that the process is at least as important as the results in these cases, and when we focus on the process at least as seriously as the results, we have a better chance of coming out with fewer scars.

A teenager negotiates with his parents because it is a means of engaging with them in a real give-and-take. We have so little in common with them in terms of interests (music, food, clothing styles, and so on) that the negotiation process is a wonderful opportunity for us to deal with each other and build the relationship.

## My Job Is Unrewarding, but My Husband Won't Let Me Change

### From: Fleur, Pondicherry, India

**Question:** *I've been working for several years with a multinational company. Currently I am looking for an easier option, as the hours are way beyond those stipulated. My husband is against the idea of my leaving this firm, as jobs these days are hard to come by. I need help in convincing him to explore other options. Also, please advise if this is a good idea in the first place!*

**Response:** The first question you have to answer is whether to negotiate with your company or your husband. Does your company have a regular quarterly or annual review process? Is there a human resources department you can talk to? Does this possibility seem less daunting than negotiating with your husband? If you have reason to conclude that negotiating with the company is not likely to yield positive results, then you do indeed need to reach agreement within the family.

I would suggest that you use your network of friends, colleagues, and schoolmates to help you get a clearer sense of the job market. You need to determine whether you are better off staying in the same field or if changing professions would offer more opportunities. Once you have a clearer idea of the likelihood of finding a more appealing job, you will have a better sense of how to respond to your husband's concern about the tight job market.

When you talk with your husband, you need to ask him a lot of questions that do not require yes-or-no answers—for example: "How would you feel if I worked better hours (and could devote more time to our relationship and family)?" You might also want to find out whether it would enhance your husband's image to have a wife who demonstrates her talents by getting a better job. Just giving up may be a simple solution, but it may well lead to bad psychological consequences for you. Your top interest is your own well-being, and your husband certainly has more to gain from having a happy wife than one who comes home from work dispirited, frustrated, or bored.

Don't view the discussions at home as "standing up to" your husband. He is your partner and has an interest in your combined income, your psychological state, and his status as someone whose wife is a professional success. If you say "Those so-and-so's at work treat me without respect; they pay me less than I deserve," and then you can add, "If you had this situation and complete freedom vis-à-vis the job market, what would you do?" Another alternative is to say, "We have a problem: my job is unsatisfactory and it is making me grumpy. How can we act as partners to solve this?"

---

## Dealing With a Stubborn Husband

### From: Shabana, Mumbai, India

**Question:** *I do not know how to deal with my husband. He is extremely introverted and very stubborn. When he gets stuck on an idea he forces me to follow it, and I am unable to get my way at all. Basically, when he becomes this stubborn, I feel powerless to even explain my viewpoint. I feel frustrated and give up. What do I do?*

**Response:** There are a number of approaches you can take. In the worst case, you could just accept that the situation is extraordinarily difficult. Then, rather than thinking of yourself as "winning" by maximizing your gains, perhaps the best thing would be to satisfy yourself by aiming to minimize your losses.

It is possible to take a more positive approach, however. You should examine your interests, prioritizing the ones that are most important to you. For example, perhaps you are most concerned about decisions that deal with children, money, or issues relating to your personal independence. The issues that are most important to you deserve the greatest effort. You might want to be prepared to trade "losses" on other interests or issues for "wins" on the more important ones.

You also need to take a look at your BATNAs regarding the issues that concern you. BATNA is your Best Alternative to a Negotiated Agreement. For example, ask yourself whether your husband is the most helpful decision-making partner on a given issue. Perhaps a friend or relative can offer you better help or resources for dealing with a particular problem. Again, taking a pessimistic view, perhaps what you need to do is consider marginalizing your husband when it comes to certain issues. Simply go your own way, to the extent you are able, and don't include him in the decision-making process. The troublesome element of this is that in some countries, there is great inequality between men and women, and this may mean that your freedom of decision and action is extremely limited. But even in that case, being able to discuss things with friends and relatives, creating a personal support group, may ease your burden.

If your husband is threatened by interaction with other people, would he feel relieved if you were to become the spokesperson for the two of you in certain kinds of activities? If he says, for example, "The telephone company is impossible to deal with," perhaps you can offer to be the person who deals with the telephone company.

You also have to ask yourself a very hard question: is the relationship so damaging to you that it is bad for you to continue in it? If that is the case, you need to examine your alternatives. If it brings you stress or health problems, even undertaking a regular program of meditation or exercise could contribute to a more rewarding inner life for you. I am recommending that you look at how you can create a situation in which you take power over elements of life that really only involve you and in which your husband has little or no interest.

When you do deal with him, listen closely to what he says:

- If what he says is not clear, keep asking questions to find out what underlies his approach.

- If what he says is unacceptable to you, respond with what Americans call a "poker face"—keep silent and don't respond; threaten him with your silence so he will know that you are not happy.

- Don't simply wait for him to stop talking and then let loose with a barrage of arguments.

- When he finishes talking, you can say, "I want to make sure I understood you properly. Did you say [x, y, and z]?" Let him know you are listening, and make it clear that the rules of discussion involve reciprocity: "I listened to you, now it is your turn to pay attention to me."

- Ask your husband about the short- and long-term consequences of his decisions. How will this approach work in six months, one year, 10 years? What results will it bring? Again, pay close attention to the things he finds most significant and try to design your responses to show that you are listening closely and understand his interests.

It sounds like your life is extremely stressful. Rather than trying to change your husband, your first priority must be to build up your personal psychological, relational, and even material resources.

---

## My Relatives Moved in, and Now They Won't Move Out

### From: Bill, Sausalito, California

**Question:** *How can I ask my relatives who are living with me right now to move out of my house without hurting their feelings? I need them to move out soon because my kids are growing up and we need more space for our own family. Right now we have 11 people living in my house and it's been more than three months since I told them that I need my rooms back and they need to look for another place soon.*

*They keep saying that they are looking for a place, but I'm not sure if that's true. When they found a place with affordable rent, they said the place was not good enough, and they would rather pay more to find a better place. (In fact, the place they found was quite good, given its price, and it was a lot better than other places we had seen in this market.) But when they find one that is advertised with a bit higher rent, they said it's too high. Every weekend, when there are new listings in the paper, they don't take a serious look at what's available. They don't make the effort to call and find out about new offerings.*

*Overall, it appears to me that they don't want to move, and they don't seem to be actively seeking for the new place. They want to get something in good condition, in a good area, and with low rent, but this seems a bit unrealistic, especially in this housing market. Given their expectations and needs, I don't know when they will ever find a place of their own to move into! In the meantime, I'm very frustrated, because there are a lot of things we need to work on in our house, which we have to put off until they move out. What can I do to make them act quickly?*

**Response:** It sounds as if you have already exhausted the classic negotiation alternatives. Negotiation requires pursuing your own interests. If you care about the relationship more than possession of your house, then you have to accept the idea that you've got permanent guests. If they care about the relationship, they must understand your interest in having your home for your own family. Let them know your feelings: that their treating you as a patsy they can take advantage of makes you feel lousy.

If they still refuse to move after you give them a clear indication of how important it is to you, perhaps you might take more drastic measures:

1. Give them a deadline: "If you are still living here after July 1, you will have to pay (very high) rent to my family." Or: "If you are still living here after July 1, I will have to take serious steps to get you to leave."

2. If the deadline passes, explain that your immediate family needs the whole house. Then move all their possessions into one room and install locks for all the other rooms in the house—perhaps even including the kitchen and bathroom(s). Tell them that if they are not gone by August 1, you will move their possessions out of the house into a storage facility (but recognize the risk you take if any of their goods are damaged).

3. When you indicate there is a deadline, you must be prepared to enforce it—otherwise you will lose credibility.

This is skirting the edge of civilized behavior. You need to think very hard about whether you are prepared to take such a "tough-guy" approach.

---

## Convincing Elders to Accept Care

### From: Naomi, Philadelphia, Pennsylvania

**Question:** *As a hospital/geriatric social worker, both in my personal and work life, I am frequently asked the following question: "My elderly [parent, aunt, neighbor] clearly needs some help at home, but refuses this help [even if free, done by a family member, a church, and so on]. How can I convince this person to accept help?" After I've determined that the issue isn't financial (which is usually a solvable problem), I am frequently at a loss. The situations I've seen like this seem to only resolve after a crisis occurs and the person has no choice.*

*How would you approach a situation like this? The issues seem to revolve around pride, retaining control, denial of illness, and aging or disability. Any thoughts?*

**Response:** In his *Notes From the Underground*, Dostoevsky wrote, "Human behavior is motivated by the craving for absolute freedom and self-assertion in defiance of all dictates of reason." As decrepitude takes its toll on our bodies and minds, often pride is the only thing we have left. Waiting for a crisis is excruciating for people who think of themselves as caregivers when it comes to organizing care for people who have a diminishing capacity to take care of themselves or their personal surroundings.

Probably the wisest thing to do is ask a whole lot of questions. Using the example of children of an elderly parent, the concerned children first need to ask themselves what their own interests are. Do they want to assuage their feelings of guilt? Do they fear that harm will come to their parent? Are they concerned that a crisis will interrupt the normal course of their own lives? Questions also need to be asked of the parent: "What most concerns you about your situation? Your health, comfortable surroundings, companionship, your capacity to hold your head up and say, 'I can do it myself!'?" You can also ask, "What, in your opinion, are the standards that determine one's capacity to live an independent life?"

This questioning approach brings all parties into fuller participation in the decision-making process. When I ask you a question, it means I am taking you seriously; the reverse is equally true. Of course, the crucial element is listening closely to all the elements of the responses to those questions, both the questions one asks oneself and the questions asked of other people. Clinging on to the indicia of independence is a critical vital sign. The fear of loving relatives that something bad can happen has to be balanced against the knowledge that if you kick someone in their self-esteem, you are attacking a most vulnerable part of their anatomy. You cannot negotiate away a person's self-esteem, but you can destroy it through frontal and flanking attacks. The frustration faced by people who see loved ones failing to take proper care of themselves is phenomenal. Very often the ones who have advocated professional care must utter the ultimate, but unsatisfying statement, "I told you so."

In your question you indicate that crisis forces choice. Perhaps the best approach is to prepare a safety net that is ready when the crisis occurs. It cannot prevent a crisis from happening, but it is crucial to make sure that a crisis is not worsened by forcing the victim to lose face. Having that safety net ready can at least reduce the force of the fall.

Relationship is one of the most significant issues to consider in negotiation. Focusing on the relationship with an elderly parent or friend, not letting decrepitude get in the way of love and caring, can make it much easier when someone's self-esteem is attacked by a crisis. Looking at oneself and saying, "It's not my fault," is not a way of avoiding blame, but rather giving a loved one the freedom to make their own mistakes—just as they did, the first time they gave us the keys to the family car.

---

## My Husband and I Communicate Badly

### From: Hasna, Cairo, Egypt

**Question:** *My husband and I are deeply in love, but the problem is that he doesn't seem well-versed in the art of speaking kind words to me. He just criticizes me because he wants everything I do to be perfect. If I do anything wrong, it's like the most horrible crime in the world. Please advise me on how I should deal with him (bearing in mind that I love him very much).*

**Response:** You are not alone in your problem. Communication between people who have a deep emotional relationship is especially difficult because everything that is said or done means more than it would in a casual situation. There are real differences between men and women; these can be minimized or heightened, depending on the culture. It is important not to embarrass your husband, but he has the same obligation not to hurt your feelings.

Before you discuss this situation with him, think about what is most important to you; then think about the things that mean the most to him. Ask him if your assumptions about his concerns are accurate. For example, does he want a "perfect" wife so his friends will have more admiration for him? If he says yes, ask him how he would describe a perfect wife. Ask him what he would do if he were you. Ask him how he feels when he learns that you are unhappy. You need to let him know that you take everything he says to you very seriously and that his criticisms make you feel bad.

Offer to bargain with him: "If you will tell me you love me four times a day, I will accept four criticisms a day without feeling hurt." "If you tell your friends (in front of me) that I am a wonderful person, it will make any private criticism hurt me less." I am sure you can imagine a whole series of bargains you can make with him. Use the "if/then" formula; always try to trade one thing for another. Remember that a husband who praises his wife in public is letting the world know that he was wise to marry her. A husband who praises his wife in private is helping her justify her love for him. The same is true about a wife praising her husband, of course.

These ideas are only the tip of the iceberg, but hopefully they will help with your situation.

---

## Choosing Between Daddy and Me

### From: Lennie, Worcester, South Africa

**Question:** *My fiancée is in another country. She didn't tell me that she was planning on leaving—well, she was supposed to go to another town, but now she's in Swaziland! I need a way of convincing her to come back. She wants to stay another two weeks, but I'm getting relocated at work, and I need her to come home now to go with me.*

*Her father totally disagrees with me, and has even started threatening me. She listens to him but not to me. Yesterday morning she told me that she would come home on Saturday, and last night (when her dad was present) she told me that she had to stay for another two weeks. Please help me to negotiate this properly, to convince her to come home.*

**Response:** You describe a difficult problem, but you are also creating one that needs to be reconsidered.

Your insistence that your fiancée choose between you and her father creates an ultimatum that carries a lot of risk for you. Although two weeks may seem like an eternity, it may well be that she must do something symbolic to obey her father before he will feel it is okay for her to return to you. Don't ask her to make her father lose face, particularly in front of you. That only adds to her stress and is not likely to make her any fonder of you.

A good relationship reflects a comprehension of the stresses and conflicts that each partner faces in life. If everything your fiancée does is supposed to revolve around you—or her father—that gives her no freedom. Should her choice reflect deciding between relationship with you or obeying her father, it means her choice does not necessarily reflect a focus on her own needs and interests.

Don't push it; it will only build resistance and risk spoiling the relationship. Control your emotions; don't let them control you.

---

## I Shouldn't Have Done It, but What Can I Do Now?

### From: Tim, Winnipeg, Canada

**Question:** *I was unfaithful to my wife before we got married, and she found out about it. The other woman (OW) means and meant nothing to me, but my wife refuses to believe that; she wants to believe the absolute worst-case scenario. I didn't have a relationship with the OW, but we did sleep together a few times.*

*Apparently the OW was upset with the fact that I wouldn't meet up with her anymore, because she found my wife's address (my fiancée at the time—she knew I was engaged by the way) and mailed her a letter detailing everything that had happened. She also included some incriminating photos.*

*I love my wife with all my heart, and I really don't know why I did it. I wasn't really attracted to the OW, she couldn't offer me anything that I didn't already have. The only thing was that I was alone at the time. While my then-fiancée was back in our hometown planning the wedding, I was in the Army stationed far away. We did the long-distance relationship for two years, and then I screwed up right at the end. My fiancée and I were arguing about the plans, and I really was alone with no one to turn to. I know this isn't an excuse for the infidelity, but I really have no other explanation for what happened.*

*Anyway, I love my wife, and I want to know how I can show her that in spite of what has happened. I want to make a new start and prove that my love for her is unending. I don't want to lose her, but we fight about this every three days or so. I think that she is thinking about divorce because of how much we fight. I just need some advice on how to talk with her about this when she brings it up, without letting it explode into another brawl. I know that, deep inside, she loves me, too, but she is hurt. I want to soothe that hurt before we end something that could be perfect. I need to hurry before she runs from me to escape the hurt. Please help me save my marriage.*

**Response:** Let's look at this situation strictly from the position of analyzing the negotiation process. Your wife is giving you a very strong message or group of messages; your job is to understand what messages she is sending and to respond appropriately.

Before your next conversation about your infidelity during your engagement, you should think about the interests, the underlying motivations that are important to you, your wife, your families, and others who have a stake in the outcome of the relationship. Try to figure out the priorities of those interests for each stakeholder. Remember that when you make those initial assumptions about what is important to whom, you are running the risk that your assumptions may not be accurate. The negotiation process offers you a chance to do a reality check on your assumptions. Once you have prepared for your next conversation, you will have a list of questions in your mind to ask to find out whether your assumptions are accurate; whatever you learn should help you respond in a way that should lead to a wise resolution of the problems.

For example, your question indicates you have assumed your wife may want a divorce. If that is one of your assumptions, you need to think very hard to come up with a series of questions that will help you find out whether you have assumed accurately. And, if your wife actually wants a divorce, does she want it because she doesn't feel you love her, because she feels she can live better under other circumstances, because her ego has been bruised, or some other reason? In other words, is your premarital infidelity the root cause of her dismay, or has she found that being married to you is not rewarding and she simply wants an excuse for ending the relationship?

No matter what you do, you must listen attentively to your wife. When you ask questions, make sure they can't just be answered with a yes or no. Use questions to search for information; what you learn may give you insights into what really counts in your wife's mind. Throughout the process you should keep your own interests in mind, as well. Don't ask anything or suggest anything that you will regret later.

Please note that I am expressing no opinion on right or wrong, but only suggesting that you have to pursue a better understanding of your wife's interests and your own. When she raises the issue of your premarital infidelity, rather than defending it or coming up with some sort of cross-accusation, let her know how you feel and ask her what she would do in your circumstances. Ask her what you would do or want her to do if the shoe were on the other foot. If you listen carefully to her words, pay close attention to her gestures; perhaps they will give you hints of a way to resolve the dilemma. Unless the two of you come up with a collaborative process for solving the problem, it won't go away.

---

## My Son Hired Me but Treats Me Like a Dummy

### From: Kathie, Easthampton, New York

**Question:** *I have been in the bar business for 20 years, working my way up from bartender to general manager for the past eight years. In those eight years I was very successful at making my former boss quite a wealthy man. In turn, he also paid me a very large salary for my skills.*

*Recently my son bought a bar, and my job now is to manage the place. My salary is now one-third of what it was. I might add that the liquor license is also in my name. Since I have been there, which is only two weeks now, my relationship with my son has turned into a nightmare. He doesn't respect my ideas, is undermining me in front of the other employees, and basically treating me as though he's doing me a favor by having me there. He openly contradicts me and makes me feel as though I don't know what I'm doing. My son is successful in running another business (not a bar). When I got involved in his new bar, his promise to me was to let me run this bar with a pay increase as profits rise, which it has done already.*

*I need to know how to deal with him as I'm very unhappy and about ready to walk out. He is not allowing me to do what I know how to do best.*

**Response:** You need to take a look at the elements of your BATNA (Best Alternative to a Negotiated Agreement) before you decide what to do. Deciding to walk out is a clear way to exercise your BATNA—once you know what it is.

Do you have a written agreement with him? If there is a written agreement, then there is language which governs the employment—and ownership—relationship. It will tell each of you what your obligations are. You indicate the liquor license for the bar is in your name. Is there any paperwork which gives your son real ownership of the license? For example, does he have a mortgage on the license which indicates you have to repay him, or that he can take the license from you for any particular reason? Or, do you own the license because there is a reason your son could not have a license in his name?

Some other important questions to ask:

- Would your former employer take you back if you were to quit working in your son's bar?

- Why did you make the change? Were you unemployed? Would you have difficulty getting a similar job someplace else? Was it your intention to do your son a favor?

- What would happen to your son's bar if you left? Who could he find to run it? Would you still control the license and be entitled to income from the business?

Once you've looked at all of these issues, you have to face the toughest one of all: how will whatever happens next impact your relationship with your son? What is your most important interest in this situation (relationship, income, status, respect from your son and/or other employees of the bar, and so on)?

Once you know what options are open to you, you should be ready to initiate a conversation with your son to bring about whatever changes you decide to pursue. Look at all the interests and the relative balance of power between you and your son. After you've determined your priorities, if you have done a good job of preparation, the negotiation process should be aimed at achieving those priority interests. If you are well-prepared, your negotiation should yield a better result.

---

## Am I a Dictator or Daddy?

### From: Lefter, Tirana, Albania

**Question:** *I am 47 years old and need some advice how to get my daughter to understand me better. She is 20 and we don't get along very well. Sometimes she doesn't respect me as I would like; sometimes it feels as though she thinks I'm basically a dictator in our family. Your advice on how to negotiate this situation would be appreciated.*

**Response:** The deeper the relationship is, the greater the likelihood that communication will be more emotionally charged. So the first thing you and your daughter should do is congratulate yourselves for the depth of your relationship—and recognize that you need to put all of your communication in that context.

It is crucial in communicating/negotiating with your daughter—or anyone else to whom you want to show respect—to make sure you spend more time listening and less time talking. There is an old expression: "God gave us two ears and one mouth. We should use them in that ratio." When you ask your daughter questions, the questions should not demand a yes-or-no answer. Ask questions that will give your daughter the opportunity to reveal what is important to her. Dictating the form of answer you want limits the likelihood she'll feel comfortable responding.

In your question's second sentence you express concern about how your daughter understands you. It is far more important to figure out how to understand her. Fathers and daughters can have extraordinarily difficult times understanding each other; if you focus on understanding her, she will reach the conclusion that you are interested in her and her opinions rather than interested in how she feels about you. I recall a true story a friend of mine told me about his dinner with a famous American statesman who is well-known for being egocentric. At first, the statesman discussed himself and his career and politics in the States. Then he said to my friend, "But we are in France, and should talk about France. Tell me, what would you say the average Frenchman thinks about me?" If you want to be a good "statesman" with your daughter, you should not make that mistake.

More than likely, you and your daughter have very different ideas about the world—different tastes in music and other entertainment, fashion, and even her choice of friends. If you recognize that the differences do not prove that one of you is better than the other, that being different is not the same as being inferior or superior, that gives you more flexibility in your responses.

Parents cannot "win" negotiations with their children. If one party wins and another party loses, the "loser" is likely to become grumpy and disinterested in reaching or fulfilling an agreement. The test of a successful negotiation is that it should be a process that yields an agreement each party will willingly fulfill. You and your daughter do share at least one critical long-term interest: you have an interest in being on good terms with each other. Look at each negotiation with her as an episode in an ongoing relationship. Ask yourself, *How does the way I communicate strengthen the bonds of love between us? How does it demonstrate that I want a mutually satisfying, long-term relationship?* This isn't easy. If you think about your behavior toward your daughter ahead of time and recognize that her respect for you will not be based on her respect for your power or your capacity to push her around, perhaps things will improve.

# He's Generous to a Fault

## From: Archna, Kuwait City, Kuwait

**Question:** *My husband is very stubborn and very generous at the same time. We are Indians who live in Kuwait. He has a bad habit of lending out money to people and then forgiving the debt. He does all this without consulting me, saying he "cannot say no" when other human beings are in need. Now that I am seven weeks pregnant, I want to keep my life as happy and stress-free as possible, but this situation is making that difficult, if not impossible. We cannot have a discussion about this. Whenever I try to bring it up, he says, "Think about something good. Don't bother yourself with such small matters." We don't talk about it when emotions are running high, but later on, if I try, he says, "I do not want to talk" or "I do not remember what happened" or even "I never said that." I am worried that these people will keep on asking and he will keep on giving. (We both are working, but that's not the issue.) What should I do to negotiate a positive outcome with my husband?*

**Response:** You need to put all the issues you've raised into context. The first step is to prioritize the things that are important to you (for example, good health, a comfortable pregnancy, continued prosperity, a good relationship with your husband, and so on). You should also take a cold-blooded, analytical look at what drives your husband's decisions. His generosity sounds a bit extreme and perhaps not always wise—but if you do have a good deal of money, maybe the funds he "lends" do not really threaten your lifestyle.

Try to figure out what drives your husband's decisions about money: Is he altruistic? Does he want to develop the reputation of a generous and good friend/relative? Does he want people to think he is rich so that he will derive other benefits? Is he trying to assuage some guilt he feels from his past when he was not able to be generous?

Most importantly, you need to choose the issues you're going to be upset about as well as the ones you're prepared to argue about with your husband. Can you trade your acquiescence regarding his "loans" for his agreement to do things you want—for example, while he builds his reputation as a generous man, could he also build his reputation as a wise man for having chosen a wonderful wife by the way he talks to you in front of others and in private conversations?

There are other possible trade-offs. You could get him to agree to set aside an equal amount of money as the amount he plans to lend for your children's education, your retirement savings, or a holiday to some attractive destination. Thus, if he lends a neighbor $1,000, he must also put the same amount of money in a special savings account for something the two of you have both agreed you want. Find things you can agree on, and think of incentives you can offer him for respecting your concerns. Your relationship's health, as well as your own comfort with the situation, may depend on your creativity in figuring out where you have influence and how to use it.

There may be things you cannot change. You need to figure out what you can accept and where there is a line that should not be crossed. Before you draw lines, however, consider what alternatives you have. Empty threats cost credibility.

---

## My Marriage Is Overpopulated

### From: Prem, Chennai, India

**Question:** *I recently got married. My wife is a doctor and I am a software engineer. Of late there has been too much interference in the marriage from my father-in-law. He has been accusing me of not taking good enough care of his daughter and is always in a high state of paranoia.*

*My wife verbally abuses me and claims that I haven't provided for her sufficiently for her to be happy. On the contrary, I arranged for the initial payment in cash for her post-graduate studies. She has even asked for a second house, which I also provided. I am earning a good salary, more than enough to provide us with a very decent standard of living. Despite her degree in medicine, my wife doesn't work at all. To make matters worse, her father claims that my father, mother, and I are harassing my wife for money, which is untrue. He even telephones my parents at midnight and abuses them. I started responding to my father-in-law's nastiness in kind in order to finish what he has started, but it hasn't seemed to work.*

*How do I handle such people (my wife and my father-in-law)? In spite of repeated requests not to poke his nose into my family life, my father-in-law doesn't listen. My wife asserts that she can't be responsible for her father's actions. How do I go about negotiating a resolution?*

**Response:** You are describing an escalating spiral of (verbal) violence with no indication of which side took the original wrong step that has led to this extraordinarily ugly situation. Escalating verbal abuse guarantees greater difficulty in finding a mutually acceptable resolution.

Your first step should be to examine what you want—not what you don't want. If your underlying objective is to have a happy marriage, you need to figure out what you mean by a "happy marriage." Simply defining happiness as the disappearance of abuse (in either direction) may be a bit shortsighted. Examine your interests and try to get a clear understanding of the options available to you (what negotiators call your BATNA, or Best Alternative to a Negotiated Agreement). How much do you have to gain or lose by taking a decisive step in any direction?

You also have to develop as clear an understanding as possible of your wife's interests and her BATNA. If the two of you can focus on your interests in your conversations, it may well be that external factors can be handled more satisfactorily. For example, if each of you feels that being free of parental intrusion would be favorable, perhaps you should consider moving to another location. Both computer engineers and doctors are likely to be able to find new jobs more easily than those in other professions.

If you and your wife are motivated to be happy together, perhaps you can take small steps to de-escalate the issues about which you have been arguing. Getting away from both sets of parents might help—but one short-term option is for you to speak only with your parents and your wife to speak only with hers. A related task is for each of you to then "forget" to deliver unfriendly messages sent along by one set of parents to you or your wife or the in-laws.

You should have different standards for the behavior of your wife and her father. Hopefully you and she can interact on a favorable level, but perhaps you should expect her father to misbehave. That way, whenever he does something unpleasant, you can congratulate yourself for predicting it—and when he is behaving nicely, you can be pleasantly surprised. It may be wise for your parents to get a new phone number if they don't want late-night harassing phone calls.

Another approach you ought to consider is to figure out how to minimize your losses. If things are only going to go downhill, you need to figure out how to protect yourself from unfortunate consequences.

Sadly, it sounds as if the situation has been handled very badly, and achieving a happy result will require a radical use of creativity on both of your parts. If the two of you are motivated to work together, you will succeed. If either or both of you are only interested in continuing the battle, the end doesn't look promising. Analyze your interests and yourself. Do the same with your wife. Ask questions to find out whether your assumptions are accurate and then proceed accordingly.

# Chapter 3

# It's Not Personal; It's Business

## Negotiation in Business Communication

### From: Masud, Colombo, Sri Lanka

**Question:** *How are negotiation skills useful in business communication?*

**Response:** Business negotiation is a process by which parties exchange information to find answers to a variety of questions, such as:

- What do you have that will help me achieve my objectives?
- What do I have that will help you achieve your objectives?
- What is the value of the ideas or items we can exchange, in terms of money and other measures of value?
- What alternatives do we have to working with each other?
- Who needs whom more?
- How will any business decision we make have an impact on other stakeholders?
- Will other stakeholders be pleased or disgruntled by the agreement we reach?

- Can you propose a better way of doing things than I propose, and vice versa?
- Who makes the decisions in each party's organization?

The list of questions can continue indefinitely. Fundamentally, negotiation is all about the exchange of information. The process by which information is exchanged is communication. Unless communication is clear and each party understands what the other party is saying, writing, or otherwise communicating, it is not possible to reach an agreement that will really reflect the objectives of the parties.

In many European languages, the word for business has the same root as the word "negotiate." Business involves trading ideas and assets—in a word, negotiation. Without good communication, business cannot succeed.

## Should I Take It or Leave It?

### From: Jim, Fresno, California

**Question:** *I am about to receive a job offer from a company that has a reputation for making "take it or leave it" offers. How should I negotiate with them? Should I negotiate with them?*

**Response:** Your first steps should involve asking yourself a number of questions: Do I want this job? What kinds of elements of a compensation package would be appropriate for me—salary, retirement plan, paid vacation time, insurance benefits, company car, office with a window, company-supplied laptop computer, flexible hours, ability to work from home, day care for a young child, frequent salary review, and so on? Another consideration is whether this is the only likely employer for you in this field and this geographical area. Perhaps another quite acceptable alternative can be found. And if you do find an alternative ahead of time, that gives you more bargaining power, particularly in the form of self-confidence.

In addition, you need to find a way to communicate to your future employer that you are concerned about negotiation styles. For example, if they have a "take it or leave it" approach toward employees, do they take this same approach with clients or suppliers? And if they do, is this the right business approach for you—and for them?

Rather than simply opening yourself to an offer that appears to require a flat yes or no, you should approach the conversation as an opportunity to learn about the job and the company by asking as many open-ended questions as you can. Even if they say "Here's the salary we offer. Do you accept, or do you want to forget about working here?" you can ask them how they would advise you to sell yourself, your spouse, or your friends on the offer they have presented. If they simply say, "That's your problem," that is a good time to give more serious thought to a possible alternative. In negotiation, if people take advantage of you from the start, it is likely to get worse in the future.

Like you, I'm sure the people at this company think of themselves as good guys who don't mean any harm. Somehow, you need to communicate to them that there are good guys on *both* sides of the bargaining table.

---

## She Sabotages My Efforts and Creates Risk for My Patients and Staff

### From: Gert, Harrisburg, Pennsylvania

**Question:** *I work in the mental health field as the supervisor of a group home. The home has two young men with difficult behaviors, and at times they can be very dangerous to work with. I have a coworker who seems to sabotage every effort my team members and I make to be consistent with these two men in trying to make their lives better. It's like we go four steps forward and two steps back whenever she's involved.*

*I feel that she is not a team player. When I tried talking to her about this during a meeting, she simply walked out. Do you have any suggestions on how to deal with her? I learned a long time ago that being consistent really helps people live better lives.*

**Response:** If this troublesome coworker is working against the proper operation of the group home in a way that creates risk for home residents or staff, you have to ask whether it is appropriate to keep her on. While you may face problems recruiting staff, and while the home may be subject to civil service rules, it is your obligation to both the staff and the residents to protect them from risk.

As supervisor you should be conducting regular performance reviews of your staff. It might be helpful to ask all staff members to provide anonymous assessments of patients and other staff members, as well as suggestions for improvements. You could use any data you receive in this process to organize your thoughts for your performance review of your troublesome staff member. Your problem staffer may have difficulties outside of work that have an impact on her work and her attitude. Perhaps a mental health professional should do an assessment of all members of the staff to help you determine whether anyone is likely to act contrary to good practice. Ultimately you need to consider the interests of all the stakeholders: yourself, the residents, and other staff. Is it in their interest to continue dealing with this person? If you are the only one she clashes with, maybe you should consider looking to someone you both trust to help facilitate a peace treaty.

You should also consider your BATNA, your Best Alternative to a Negotiated Agreement. If you are stuck with keeping her on staff, can you assign her to work that keeps her from sabotaging the overall operation of the group home? If you are not compelled to keep her on, both you and she may be better off ending the relationship.

---

## She Leaves Her Work for Me to Do

### From: Juliet, Madison, Wisconsin

**Question:** *I have been having some problems with a coworker. She is a very slow worker and I work quickly. I've been working with her for almost two years and it seems she takes advantage of the fact that I work quickly. She will leave things undone knowing that I will do it.*

*I work in a school kitchen and if these jobs don't get done, the kids are the ones who suffer. I told her how I felt, and now she isn't speaking to me. I don't feel that I did anything wrong by standing up for myself. Did I do the right thing? She asked me to be honest with her. My only mistake is that I let it go on too long without saying anything.*

**Response:** If your coworker asked you to be honest with her, unless you used inappropriate language, your answer was fundamentally the right thing to do.

When things bother you, if you don't assert yourself early in the situation when issues are relatively small, problems escalate and get tougher to solve. While you may take some blame on yourself for having waited too long to raise the issues, the fact is your coworker has been letting you down, probably doing the same to other members of the staff, and creating the risk that the kids may not get the service they deserve.

You should approach your coworker and indicate that you have a very real interest in a harmonious work atmosphere. Ask her how she feels about that issue and what thoughts she has about the problems you raised. Listen closely to her answers for hints of how best to communicate with her. What is important to her? What are her hot buttons? You need to let her know that you are upset with yourself for not having spoken up earlier, but that since she asked for your honesty, it would have been disrespectful to withhold your true feelings.

If she refuses to communicate with you, you need to consider your alternatives. Has she changed her work habits? Do you have a supervisor who can give the two of you separate assignments so it is clear who is doing the job and who is falling behind? Are there other people in your crew with whom you can strengthen your relationships to build your support network?

---

## How Long Can She Treat Me Like This?

### From: Jan, Eden, North Carolina

**Question:** *Because the company I work for is so small, there are only a total of eight employees. I have been working there for about a year and a half.*

*Recently one of my coworkers has begun taking out her frustrations on me. She has a lot going on at home and is, by nature, a worrier. She is 30 years older than me and, I guess, intimidated by the fact that I learned her job in about eight months. She has been here longer than me, and I respect her, but it's getting harder and harder to let things slide when she makes ugly remarks to me in front of the other employees.*

*I get along great with everyone else, as does she, but there is something about me she doesn't like. I have spoken with my boss about this; he thinks that she'll chill out after a while, but it's been going on for about five months.*

*I love my job and don't want to quit, but I can't take her being this ugly to me all the time. What do I do?*

**Response:** You indicate an understanding that your difficult colleague has problems at home, worries a lot, and is threatened by the speed with which you have acquired skills that may have taken her more time. There may be other factors that you need to consider as well: is the difference in age and seniority peculiar to the two of you, or are other coworkers similarly spread out in terms of age and experience?

Can you put yourself in her shoes and consider any nervousness she may feel about keeping her job, or differences in taste that cause her to feel uncomfortable? If you like different clothing, music, food, and topics of conversation, could these be a cause of offense? If you are offending her, that doesn't mean you're wrong to have your own tastes, but it may be wise to consider how it makes her feel.

You don't indicate how communication works between you and your nemesis. Does she speak directly to you, and do you fight back? Do you say something such as, "When I hear someone talk that way about me, it makes me feel hurt/embarrassed/unappreciated." Have you considered taking the initiative by going to her for advice (even if you don't really need it): "How would you handle this? Can you give me advice about this customer/supplier/process?"

Conversations about feelings can be very important. Put yourself in her shoes and ask her to do the same: "How would you feel/react if someone said this?" Gestures like going for coffee may help assuage her insecurities about you. She may view you as having powers she doesn't have as a younger person, a faster learner, or whatever. She may appreciate hearing you say that getting along with her is really important to you because you value her understanding of the company. This takes imagination and creative thought, diplomacy, and perhaps even some acting skills.

Being honest about your feelings need not be a matter of going into combat. There may be problems you can solve together, but you need to reach some agreement that those problems exist.

# She Tries to Sabotage Her Workplace Colleagues

## From: Linda, Seattle, Washington

**Question:** *I have a coworker who hoards key information so she can be the shining star when it comes to resolving issues. She is the "knowledge is power" person. For example, she doesn't inform key people of meetings, meeting outcomes, or goals. This keeps everyone having to come to her for help and advice.*

*Recently I received a long-anticipated and well-earned promotion. She was furious. She placed a call to our corporate HR person, demanded the specifics of the job description, and then proceeded to demand an interview for herself. Needless to say, this has caused quite a bit of disharmony and confusion.*

*How do I get this straightened out? While I appreciate competition in the workplace, I cannot tolerate sabotage. How can I get this behavior brought to the attention of the right people? This is not the first time she has gone after someone else's opportunity. Help!*

**Response:** Your final paragraph looks toward how to reach the desired end state of the current situation. Figuring out who the right people are is certainly the first step you should take, if indeed there are "right people" who can bring about improvement. However, before you get the information to the right people, you need to determine what your interests are and how they can be reached.

Your "saboteur" coworker sounds as if she is extremely lacking in self-confidence, even to the point of paranoia. One question is whether she performs functions on the job that are necessary to accomplish the goals of your company (or your section of the company). If you find that a sufficient number of other colleagues are prepared to marginalize her and keep her out of the loop in every possible situation, the question is whether your work output will suffer at all. Should the output be just as good without her, you can demonstrate her irrelevance and get on with fulfilling your job obligations.

Withholding information is dangerous for the company; if an employee holds back crucial information and suffers a sudden health problem or accident, that means the company's work objectives cannot be achieved. One of the benefits of teamwork—and collaborative negotiation—is that there is always backup if one of the team members is not available at a crucial time.

If your number-one goal is to have less stress in the workplace, you should examine all the choices available to you. These range from sabotaging the saboteur and developing allies who can work successfully together without her, to quitting your existing job and taking one where there is less likelihood of stress from paranoid colleagues. Assuming you are committed to doing a good job, and the work itself is rewarding, you need to consider how you can focus on what satisfies you—and your superiors and other colleagues.

Your unfriendly coworker appears to fear that anyone else's success means she is a failure. It may well be that her analysis is wrong and that, with effort, it is possible to convince her to "get her mind right" (as Paul Newman's character says in *Cool Hand Luke*). If others on the job succeed by working together and are rewarded for their cooperation with each other, that may provide positive reinforcement for the idea that collaboration is more rewarding than seeking self-aggrandizement.

Look for allies among your peers and the higher-ups. Question whether changing the way work is done or decisions are made will get you better results in terms of the saboteur. Think of the saboteur as a person who is crying for help—and look for ways to provide it. Remember the old saying "Time wounds all heels"; look at the long term and don't let short-term aggravation get you down. Use out-of-the-box thinking to find more satisfactory ways to get the job done.

---

## She Came, She Intervened, and Now She Won't Leave

### From: Teresa, Hayward, California

**Question:** *I need advice regarding a situation in my workplace. I am a closing agent in the real estate business and assistant manager in my department. My manager and I were requested by the GM (general manager) to* *allow the OM (operations manager) to come to our department and set it up to operate as a processing center. Normally, in our business, the workflow is handled differently; however, due to a high volume of closings, it was necessary to make the change.*

*The OM completed her task of reorganization a year ago. However, she will not "let go" and allow the manager and me to properly train our staff and oversee our department. How can we tactfully and skillfully tell the OM to "let go"? She is sensitive, overbearing, and feels like she must have control.*

**Response:** One wonders whether the GM wants things to stay the way they are. Did he assign the OM to work with your department to get her out of his hair? You and your department manager ought to do some research on the GM's short- and long-term objectives regarding both your department and the OM. If the OM hasn't got anything better to do than interfere in your department's work, does that indicate that there's no other work for her to do in the company?

Since the GM got you into this situation, he has an obligation to help you design and implement an exit strategy. However, if you and your department manager decide to handle the relationship with the OM on your own, it could make a great deal of sense to figure out who the stakeholders are in the situation: owners, customers, members of the administrative hierarchy, the individuals directly involved (including yourselves)—and whoever else you think should be considered. Then try to figure out what the interests are of each party; not just what they want as an outcome, but *why* a given solution would be a good way to achieve that outcome.

Prior to your face-to-face with the OM, if you have done a good job looking at the stakeholders and their interests, you should be able to come up with some creative alternatives to the existing situation that save the OM's face without making you and your manager feel like idiots, victims, bad guys, or all three. Before you communicate with the OM, you need to know what information will help you influence her decision. You also need to have a clear sense of what decisions she is empowered to make. Once you have a sense of what information you need, you can develop a series of questions to ask her that will help lead her to understand your feelings as well as your departmental needs. Asking questions is far more respectful than simply telling someone, "This is the way it is; take it or leave it."

You may want to find out whether the OM feels you and your departmental manager are demonstrating competence in the modified procedure she designed. Perhaps if you feel she's done a good job, you can offer to "sell" her services to other units of your organization that may also benefit from procedural redesign. That's one of the things you should find out from the GM before dealing with the OM. It may also be possible to ask the OM how she would feel if someone were behaving toward her as she is behaving toward you. Obviously, this must be handled diplomatically.

You need to understand how far you can go without upsetting the GM, without turning the OM into an active enemy, and without looking like crybabies. Good preparation should arm you for virtually whatever may arise in the process.

---

## We Taught Her Everything; Now She's Stealing the Credit

### From: Kelly, Gallipolis, Ohio

**Question:** *I hired someone who did not have the required experience for the job, but who (I thought) had the ability and desire to learn. I have spent six months of many hours teaching her on the job. In addition, I have used highly paid senior managers to provide many hours of on-the-job training, working with her side-by-side. She has been successful.*

*The problem occurs when I overhear others/outsiders giving her praise and compliments. She accepts the compliments as her own and has never given others credit for their help. At times she has received compliments for what I know to be others' work and, again, accepts the compliments without giving credit where it's due. This really bothers me, hurts my feelings, and probably the feelings of the people who have invested much time and effort to help her. Should I approach her about this, and, if so, how?*

**Response:** There are two factors at play here. When someone takes credit for things that other people did, their mentors might take it as a hit in the ego. We all want to get the credit we deserve, and we often resent it when others steal our thunder.

On the other hand, in a business situation, when someone is dealing with outsiders, it is awfully important to give those outsiders the impression that every member of the team is talented and can do the job well. Your business might lose credibility if she were to tell folks who compliment her, "Thanks for your nice words, but I really don't deserve them. Other folks in the company are more experienced than I and it's their work that's made me look good." That would leave outsiders with the impression that you hire people who are really not up to the job, which would only serve to take away outsiders' confidence in your company's capacity to deliver. Most people want to deal with people who come across as knowledgeable and able to deliver in terms of their job responsibilities.

In spite of that pragmatic analysis, hurting the egos of others is, at best, bad manners. Thus, you need to take a well-considered approach when you talk with this woman. You should bring her into a private conversation and begin by asking her about her progress and development on the job. Let her know that it would be helpful for your assessment of the job performance of others in the company if you could find out who she credits for contributing to her development and success. Ask her how she has acknowledged her colleagues' help—both directly, to them, and indirectly, by giving them credit in discussing the team's talents with outsiders.

Her responses will give you insight into how her mind works as well as the opportunity to let her know how important it is to the team's collective ego and consequent productivity to share credit and/or give credit where it is due. You should feel proud, knowing that you and your colleagues have taken a diamond in the rough and made her into (something approaching) a jewel. It sounds as if there are still some rough edges to smooth. If you do the job well, it will reflect well on you and the company, and improve this woman's value as a member of the team.

---

## His Dirty Hands Handle Our Food

### From: Brenda, Allentown, Pennsylvania

**Question:** *My problem relates to a coworker. He is a PhD, but he does not have the common sense to wash his hands after being in the men's room. Many of our male employees have witnessed his lack of hygiene and have reported it to our safety manager. What's worse is that this person insists on* *picking up food (we have lunch and snacks provided to us) with his fingers, no matter how many times we tell him to use a spoon, fork, tongs, and so on. Everyone here is disgusted and grossed out, and because of how easily lawsuits are filed nowadays, we aren't sure how to address this correctly without upsetting him. We are also concerned that this bad behavior could eventually cause someone to become seriously ill because of all the germs he is spreading around.*

*Can you give me any advice on the best course of action to take in dealing with this problem?*

**Response:** The first question is what your safety manager has done in response to the reports of your colleague's bad hygiene. A qualified safety manager should have been trained in how to deal with such issues. So she/he should be the first person you go to for advice.

A next step could be to address the issue of how food is prepared and distributed. If anyone can "graze" a buffet and, in so doing, touch other peoples' food with dirty hands, maybe it would solve the immediate health safety problem to have the food served in individual servings so this slob is only able to touch his own food. Another possibility is to have a sign at the start of the food line requiring everyone to use a hand-cleaning product before touching a utensil or any food due to health considerations. (This should be accompanied by a supply of hand wipes or hand sanitizer.)

These approaches do not deal with the issue of getting the PhD to clean up his act. It could make sense for one of his male colleagues who witnesses his failure to wash in the men's room to ask the slob why he doesn't perform this critical step in personal hygiene. It is important to ask questions rather than simply say, "Your personal habits are lousy." Being judgmental is not nearly as likely to get your slob to buy into the discussion as showing respect and curiosity by asking open-ended questions. People are less likely to change their attitude or behavior for negative reasons than for positive ones.

You need to find out who among the men have witnessed the PhD's poor hygiene—and how many of them are prepared to ask a simple question, "Why don't you wash your hands afterwards?" As a practical matter, even people who do wash after using the restroom are still exposed to germs and viruses on paper, telephones, and other things they touch during the normal course of the day, so it may be worthwhile to ask your safety manager to bring in a medical professional to discuss disease prevention with the staff. Given the threat of diseases spreading because so many people travel, this would probably be a good thing to do regardless of your slob's poor personal hygiene.

---

## Fear of Change Harms Our Clinic

### From: Elias, Bethlehem, Pennsylvania

**Question:** *As a manager of a large clinic I need your help in handling negative attitudes and fear of change in one of the four departments I manage. I could also use some tips in improving my interpersonal communications with the head of the department, someone who is dealing with a lot of frustration and stress. The word from his staff is that he is not handling things very well.*

**Response:** When people are afraid of change, it is crucial to try to figure out why this is the case. Are they afraid that change will cause them to lose power, to lose face, to show their colleagues that they are not capable of doing the job except in the way they've always done it?

You need to talk with your colleagues, particularly the "cooperative" heads of the other three departments you manage. Try to figure out what issues underlie the fourth department head's fear of change. Is he afraid of looking underqualified? Has he had bad experiences in the past relating to change, on the job or in other areas of life?

Look for what the departmental head has to lose, and what he has to gain by the change. Will it bring additional resources? Can he anticipate that accepting change and fulfilling the new requirements will improve his reputation within the firm, with the public, and/or with specific individuals? Find ways to ask him what he feels there is to gain from changes, and also take a serious look at where the changes may create risk. It could help if he felt as if he were contributing to increased success, and that he will get credit for his contribution to the improved delivery of services. Find out where there are common objectives, even if not everyone agrees on how those objectives should be achieved.

In response to the second part of your question, if the departmental head can be convinced to accept change, clearly that should overcome the frustration he is currently generating in his staff. However, you have to ask a hard question: if he continues to be against change and thus continues to contribute to staff frustration, are there steps that must be taken? Should he be transferred out of the clinic? Should he be given different responsibilities? Might he respond better to pressure from the staff than from his fellow heads or from the boss? The important thing is to figure out everyone's interests, including staff members and constituents (patients, patients' families, and so on). Ask open-ended questions that don't require a yes-or-no answer before you offer your own answers.

Remember that everyone has an ego. You need to figure out how to deal with whatever drives the ego of each of the parties. If you are collaborative in your approach, bringing in and respecting the ideas of others, perhaps you can overcome the uncooperative behavior of the departmental head.

---

## My New Boss Is Impossible!

### From: Trisha, Washington, D.C.

**Question:** *I have a new manager, and when he speaks to me, he gives me orders. When I try to negotiate my position with him, he gets angry and yells. He is in a position where he has four new salespeople working for him, and he has very much a "dictator" style. I am learning to ask lots of questions, but other than play to the power trip he is on, what are my hopes of negotiating with him? What is your best advice for dealing with him? (I also think he is easily threatened by managers that facilitate, as I've been told not to talk to them.) I'm very much at a loss as to how to get this to a "win-win." Please help!*

**Response:** It sounds as if you have taken the crucial first step by asking him tons of questions. That is a wise initial response. However, the situation you describe requires that you take some additional steps, as well.

When he yells, perhaps you should talk more quietly, thus forcing him to listen more closely for your reaction. It is easy to dismiss his flawed character with the diagnosis that he is on a power trip, that he is a control freak or a dictator. However, those descriptions are not diagnostic, but merely descriptive. You need to find out what the root causes of those symptoms are.

Think of a series of questions that are likely to yield a better understanding of what underlies his attitude and behavior. What is he afraid of? Whom is he afraid of? If he has told you not to talk with certain people, why is that? What could they do to him? Could they undermine his own sense of importance, his capacity to push people around? What can you find out about his behavior in prior positions? With the information you discover, perhaps you can find ways to disarm some of his uglier habits or attitudes. You may be able to anticipate the steps you can take that will mollify him without making you feel defeated.

In addition to your own personal thoughts about him, talk to others to see what they have concluded. Find out whether they have found successful ways to approach him or respond to him. Is there a discernible pattern? You might also want to figure out how best to limit your interactions with him. Can you communicate by memorandum, e-mail, or other non-in-person means? Among other things, using memos or e-mails can leave a paper trail, if he responds using the same medium.

Does he have a superior you can talk to? Would it make sense for you to change positions to get out of his turf?

Yet another approach is to leave for work every morning asking yourself, *How badly will my manager behave today?* Maybe you should mark him on a range from one to 10—if he behaves well, that's great, but if he behaves badly, then he's living down to your expectations.

It is crucial not to take such bad behavior personally. How he behaves is a reflection on him, not you. When he's being troublesome, congratulate yourself on how much more civilized you are. You deserve those congratulations.

---

## The Boss Seems Afraid to *Be* Boss

### From: Joseph, Barcelona, Spain

**Question:** *I am a new employee in a firm I will call Small Company. This company belongs to a group of companies (which I will call Big Company) with a common GM (general manager). I am the director of Small Company. Two months after I started, the GM hired a new OM (operations manager) for Big Company. I must report to this OM. The problems are as follows:*

1.  *I do not have a good rapport with this man.*

2.  *This man treats the directors with arrogance and bad manners.*

3.  *He is only concerned with delegating tasks and responsibilities. His main obsession is to arrange meetings, only to change the agenda later on.*

4.  *He is afraid to talk with the GM and yet he is unable to make decisions without talking with the General Manager beforehand. Thus, he simply prepares long-winded e-mails and memos.*

*As you can imagine, this is a very difficult situation and dis-motivational to all concerned. Any advice?*

**Response:** Your description gives me a sense the OM is very unsure of himself. Do the other directors have the same opinion of him that you have? It is important for you to find out whether the directors are in agreement. If they are, it could make sense to discuss a common strategy for improving the situation. Can the directors communicate directly with the GM without having to go through the OM?

If you are the only director (or part of a minority) who feels uncomfortable with the OM, perhaps you should examine your alternatives: would you be better off staying with the company or looking for another job? Perhaps you should stay for one year before you leave if it would look better on your employment record.

It sounds as though you don't want to change jobs, but simply want to improve the atmosphere and operations of your company. Under these circumstances you need to examine why the OM was hired: did the GM need a buffer between himself and the directors? Does the OM have a relationship with the GM, the owners of the Big Company, or political connections that make him particularly valuable?

Changing meeting agendas is certainly bad manners. It is also a poor way to make decisions. If you arrive at a meeting prepared for one set of issues and the other parties want to discuss different issues, you can't negotiate as wisely. So perhaps you want to let the OM know that if he wants the best productivity from you, using mutually accepted agendas could mean you are better prepared when you and he meet.

Can you think about all the possible reasons the OM may be behaving badly? Perhaps you'll want to discuss this with other directors. Is the OM afraid of something? Does he come from an organization that was full of paranoia, in which people had to do everything on paper to protect their reputations? If your current company did not have a paranoid environment before the OM's arrival, perhaps there are ways to increase his confidence by doing things "his way" now so that, in the future, he is more open to accepting other people's ideas.

You might find ways to develop a relationship with the OM, finding out whether your assumptions about his motives are accurate, learning more about his objectives and his preferred ways of doing things. With that information you may be able to develop a more satisfactory professional relationship. In order to do this you need to consider how much time you are prepared to invest in improving things and whether this time investment is appropriate.

To a certain extent, the OM sounds like a bully. I don't know how that would translate into Spanish. But one key characteristic of bullies is that they are afraid of failure. Perhaps you can tell the OM, "I am afraid we may fail to reach agreement." Warning him that he might be part of a failure may get his attention and help improve the situation.

---

## Convincing My Boss
## That the Company Needs Training

### From: Kate, London, England

**Question:** *How do I tell my line manager the importance of training in negotiation skills for managers and supervisors in my company?*

**Response:** Everyone negotiates in both professional and private life—and the success of those negotiations can have a profound impact on everything from personal satisfaction to corporate profitability.

Your question does not spell out the reasons you think negotiation skills training would be valuable for your company. Before trying to convince anyone of anything, it is crucial to examine what they or their organization could gain by accepting your ideas. For example, there are several possible reasons that enhancing negotiation skills could help your company, but you need to present these reasons as questions rather than as definite conclusions that you present as incontrovertible facts. A list of those questions could include the following:

- What are the best ways for the company to deal with internal conflicts among cliques that interfere with the decision-making process?
- What changes would aid the company's bottom line in terms of increased sales, better procurement policies, and more effective use of such company assets as human resources, machinery, or processes?
- How would things improve if the company used a collaborative decision-making process?
- What interests would be better served if more of the company's stakeholders were satisfied with the way the company reaches agreements with its staff, clients, suppliers, lenders, landlords, owners, and so on?

You should note that these questions don't ask for simple yes-or-no answers; they are designed to dig out information so that you can develop a clearer understanding of what drives the decisions of the people you are talking to. As you learn about what they think is important, you should be able to express reasons for initiating the kinds of training programs that will yield the results your colleagues (line manager and other decision-makers) would like to gain for the company.

---

## I'm the First Female Boss in an Oil Company

### From: Rochelle, Dallas, Texas

**Question:** *I am a woman and I work as an engineer in an oil company. My manager has given me a good position in my department (Materials) as a coordinator for the purchasing section. I am new in this position and I don't know how to deal with my employees, particularly since I am the first woman in this company who has reached this position of authority. Would you please advise me on how to negotiate with my team, especially my male subordinates, so that I can be successful in my new job?*

**Response:** You face both short- and long-term problems. The immediate need is to develop a good working relationship with your subordinates. Rather than focusing on issues relating to your own self-confidence, you may be more successful if you can help your employees feel confident that having a woman as their boss will not jeopardize their capacity to do their jobs well. Another issue is that the men working for you may not be accustomed to having a woman as their leader.

If your employees don't know much about your background, it could be helpful to have an informal discussion in which you examine the technical issues your department faces. During that discussion, you should tell your employees that although you are the boss, you know that a good boss is one who makes maximum use of the talents of her employees, and who will give them credit for their good ideas and good work. You should also describe your own background and qualifications and say, for example, "From my experience with the 'X' company, I have found that they need to be reminded about delivering according to our specifications. So far I have been successful by doing random testing. Do any of you have other ideas for making sure their product is always good enough for our company?" In other words, demonstrate your experience while letting your employees know you are open-minded.

Be careful not to communicate a message that puts you in a subordinate position. Assert your talents and skills without being aggressive. Build a cooperative mentality by inviting your subordinates to become partners in a successful team.

You should ask questions and listen closely to how people answer. If someone's answer is hostile or unproductive, rather than responding quickly with a negative statement or an indication that you are upset or embarrassed, you should put on your poker face and not say anything. Just sit—or stand—and don't show any kind of response. More than likely, the person who has troubled you will feel the need to try again, hopefully with a better attitude. If you respond to hostility with your own hostility or some expression of a lack of self-confidence, it only escalates the problem.

The long-term issues you face relate to two issues: your interactions with your superiors and your interactions with people from other companies. Your interest within the company is to demonstrate your skill, your competence, and your capacity to arrive at creative results. Keeping calm and listening for what your bosses want will let them know that you take them and the company seriously—and that you are therefore someone they should take seriously. When you are dealing with outsiders, be well-versed on the issues. Ask your colleagues what they know about the outsiders; demonstrate that you take your colleagues seriously. At the same time, listen to the outsiders, ask them questions, and then respond to what you recognize as the points they take most seriously. If it is clear to them that you understand the issues, they should treat you as a professional.

Working well with your subordinates and with outsiders should prove your value to your bosses. And behaving as a professional should keep building your reputation with your subordinates, clients, and others you do business with.

---

## They Keep Changing the Rules

### From: Young-eun, Seoul, Korea

**Question:** *I work for a Korean biotech venture company. I have been in contact with a unit in a British hospital regarding their technology. I heard that they are short on research funds, so I thought that we could negotiate with them fairly easily. I sent a proposal, offering an upfront payment of $20,000 and two percent of running royalty, and they accepted our offer.*

*However, they changed their minds and decided they wanted us to pay everything up front, instead of providing a running royalty, because they are cash-poor. We accepted it and countered with an upfront payment of $30,000. They then made a counter-offer of $80,000, saying that it was nonnegotiable.*

*I am afraid to say that we told them we really need their technology; we also didn't say that we have alternatives. What should I do? I am preparing materials that will show the market situation and expected sales and profit for our company. But will that be enough? Or do we have to find alternatives? (We've contacted several companies, but the British hospital is the only one that has shown any interest in working with us.)*

**Response:** Unless you have a written contract, I suggest you communicate with the British organization and say that you are not comfortable with the way the negotiations have been going. Indicate that you are concerned that because of possible differences relating to both national and corporate cultures, it appears that you have reached a point where the agreement is lacking clarity in terms of communication, understanding, and consequently, the elements necessary for agreement.

You need to take a close look at your company's interests and the prioritization of those interests. Most likely, your top priority is to make money—but you may also want to get a product to market, to establish your credibility, to create or expand jobs within your company, and so on. Paying attention to those interests and making certain you do not write or say anything that conflicts with your interests is your most important job in negotiation. Thus, in this case, if you conclude that your need to do business with the British organization is the more important interest, then you can draw conclusions about how much you can concede in the negotiation process.

Once you are clear on your priorities, you can then communicate your concerns to the organization in the UK. You might suggest there is a list of issues that need to be clarified or resolved if you are to do business together. You should ask them what factors are going to drive their decision. If it is already clear to you that they need to be convinced that your company has sufficient assets, which your question seems to indicate, you need to consider creative options in structuring the deal in terms of upfront cash, a form of bonding or insurance that guarantees they will be paid, or some other approach. If you have calculated the likely amount of income their product can generate for you, it could make sense to develop a price you are willing to pay them which represents a discounted proportion of the total net revenues you anticipate the product will generate.

This is a complex series of issues. You need to get your own thinking in order, comprehend your own priorities, try to get a better understanding of their priorities, and then reinvent or restart the negotiation process based on a mutual face-saving formula.

---

# I'm Irreplaceable, but My Son Wants Me to Move

### From: Jill, Riverside, Rhode Island

**Question:** *My son asked me to relocate to Oregon from Rhode Island in order to be close to the family. I've started the long, tedious relocation hassle.*

*I gave my boss of 15 years more than three months' notice, but nobody wants my job. Applicants see my heavy job description and low pay, and they run for the hills. If I decide to stay, do I have additional bargaining power? Is BATNA applicable here? How would I negotiate for a higher salary before I burn my bridges?*

**Response:** You raise two issues that appear separate, but are really intertwined. The first relates to your interest in moving closer to your family. You should ask yourself whether the proposed move is going to bring you closer to one set of very important people but may bring other changes in your life about which you are less enthusiastic. Your analysis of this will help you figure out how to deal with your decision about your current job.

As regards the job—and everything else one negotiates—BATNA is always an element. You should always consider your Best Alternative to a Negotiated Agreement—as well as the BATNAs of other negotiating parties and others with an interest in the outcome. If your boss's response is strongly aimed at keeping you on the job, if you are rewarded by your work (leaving aside issues of pay and job description for the moment), and if staying on the job in your present location might outweigh the benefits of moving closer to your family, then your focus on negotiation with your employer will be better organized.

The way to assess your bargaining power with your boss is by figuring out what information she can provide you that tells you how much she wants you to stay. You have to ask questions designed to elicit the information upon which you can base your proposals and your decisions. If she lets you know you are irreplaceable, you need to indicate that you have a very attractive alternative in Oregon and that you can only stay where you are if there are specific changes in your pay, your conditions, or other elements of the job to keep you on the team.

Raising issues like these in a polite and reasonable way—and being prepared to walk away if they don't respond favorably—is not likely to be viewed as an expression of hostility on your part. Make sure you don't put your boss in jeopardy of losing face; but make equally certain that you don't agree to anything you'll regret. You won't burn bridges, and you may put out some fires that have been troubling you for a long time.

## Healing a Relationship With a Difficult Coworker

### From: Erik, Eau Claire, Wisconsin

**Question:** *I have been trying to work with a difficult, younger coworker, who is probably intimidated by my age and experience. He is difficult to deal with for management as well as other coworkers. He plays games and exhibits immature behavior, but mostly has a problem with me. He has been counseled numerous times by management, but will not accept any responsibility for the problem; therefore, a head-on approach doesn't seem to be the answer. He and I basically avoid interaction, but I would like to have a better relationship with him to decrease on-the-job stress. Any ideas?*

**Response:** One of the most effective ways to get out of the rut that may reduce a relationship's quality is to do something surprising or unexpected. You might want to examine the general game plan of your relationship with your troublesome coworker: look at the processes you employ in your dealings with each other and compare them with your dealings and his dealings with others—both within your organization and (at least in your case) away from work.

It is crucial not to be judgmental as you review how you two relate to one another and to others on the job. Questioning who's at fault won't get you anywhere. It could be useful, however, to look for hot buttons: What drives me crazy? What drives him crazy? And, having discovered the hot buttons, it may make sense not to try to "cure" his. Just being aware of them should be enough to influence your behavior to avoid pushing those hot buttons. Understanding your own hot buttons is somewhat more difficult; it is not always easy to analyze ourselves. But you might ask, does this behavior of his also bother me when someone else does the same thing?

What do you expect/anticipate from him? What does he expect/anticipate from you? If you behave in a different way and take him by surprise, that may bring a momentary pause in the usual processes of the relationship.

There is nothing wrong in a conversation that is aimed at learning more about his interests. In my own experience, working in a philanthropic or academic organization can be extremely frustrating. The less there is to fight over, the more bitter the fights. Do you have or control any resources that could help defuse some of his frustration? Is there anything substantive he has to offer you? Forget about "Let's be friends...." The issue is to start with what diplomats call *confidence-building measures*: "If you do this, then I will do that." Or, "If I do this, then will you do that?" Take an "if/then" approach to bargaining.

Can you offer him opportunities that others cannot—the chance to choose projects to work on? The chance to join or even chair a working group? Access to information, perks, a preferred spot on the vacation schedule? Quick delivery of office supplies? Flexible work hours? An introduction to someone he would like to have access to? Early warning about opportunities, dangers, projects, or cutbacks? Inside information about a good restaurant? What interests do you have in common? Do you both work in a department dealing with issues which you are deeply committed to? Does either of you have ideas to bounce off the other to improve the system?

In your question you indicate he will not accept responsibility for problems he is having on the job. Hypothetically speaking, if you could move the problems away from being personified by him, would the problems still exist? If so, you may find common ground in trying to solve those problems. If the problems really do relate to how he gets along with fellow workers, perhaps you should accept the fact you carry little or no responsibility. It is not your job to try to "reform" him.

If his problem getting along with you is too much for you, then you should examine whether you have anything to gain from having a relationship. Who is going to be at your organization longer (not current longevity, but future)? If it looks like you're stuck with the way things are, you should plan to face the disappointment of an unrewarding relationship. Perhaps you remember Ronald Reagan's put-down of Jimmy Carter during one of their presidential debates: "There you go again." I would never say that to anyone, but you can think it to yourself and it may help calm you down.

Remember this as well: sometimes "winning" a negotiation is about minimizing your losses.

# Dealing With the Person Who Beat You Out for a Promotion

### From: Simon (management consultant), Birmingham, England

**Question:** *What approach should I take when dealing with my manager? The problem is that we were part of the same team and both applied for the supervisor's post, and after the usual interviews, he was selected. I now find he wants to change everything and throws out decisions like confetti. I appreciate that this is the norm for a new manager who wants to consolidate his role by demonstrating to his manager his competence and by showing his staff that he is assertive. Normally I pride myself that I can keep the balance between my manager's objectives, my customers', and my own. However I am finding it difficult to manage upward due, among other things, to the aggression I am feeling from my new manager.*

*Do you have any advice on how this situation is best handled? Should I go with the flow and accept change, or try and moderate some of these changes with some practical common sense? I find that it is one of the most difficult negotiations that I have been involved in and would welcome your input.*

**Response:** Your situation sounds challenging, and the way you summarize your choices is very clear. I infer from your introduction to the situation that your new manager is aware that the two of you were competing for the same job—and that he "won." Clearly this puts you in a tough spot.

Going with the flow and waiting for the smoke to clear is not wrong, but I do not think it is wise. Your communications need to establish the new relationship in a way that responds to your interests. Meeting with him privately, perhaps outside of work over a friendly drink, might offer an opportunity for you to save both your face and his while establishing necessary limits.

He needs to know that you congratulate him for his promotion, that the company was lucky to have several highly qualified candidates, and that his promotion is a real feather in his cap. You might go on to say that you hope that next time, you get the nod and that you want to do an excellent job under his leadership in order to add to your own value and simultaneously demonstrate to the powers above that their choice of him is a good one.

Without necessarily using the words, you may wish to offer to be his confidant, his sounding board, as he establishes his position in his new role. He can depend on your unbiased responses to his proposals because you will always be honest with him, realizing that even if you are not entirely in agreement with his proposed course of action, you will give 110 percent to help him realize his stated goals. By the same token, you need to be cautious not to appear to be kissing up. This is a situation of two former peers who, having been equals, must continue dealing with each other with mutual respect for each to succeed in the new relationship.

Most important, you should listen. After your congratulations, you should ask about his goals, his short- and long-term strategy, how he sees you and others contributing to the direction he wants to take. But listen. Remember your mouth can get you in far more trouble than your ears. What you learn from him now may aid your future relationship with him as well as your future prospects within the organization.

It is no great joy to lose a competition of any sort. But it is even worse to be ignored and not allowed to compete in the first place.

---

## Passed Over at Work

### From: Walter, Jacksonville, Florida

**Question:** *I have been in the environmental, health, and safety field for 15 years. I started out as an engineer, then senior engineer, and now lead engineer. Recently, a managerial position in our department became available. I was sure that after all these years of experience, intra-company management classes, and the fact that I had actually supervised employees, I would be next in line for the job. However, I was made aware very quickly that the staff did not want to work for me.*

*I was surprised that the staff was so opposed to my style. I have always been both a global and a detailed thinker. As I look back on the 10 years of working in the same department, I remember having some creative ideas that the staff rejected. There have been times when I have gotten angry because the staff was quick to reject my ideas. Once I revealed the anger in my expression and voice, all possible negotiation for the idea was generally over. This has been very frustrating to me because I have some good ideas. I've talked with someone in HR about the issue. She believes that my enthusiasm and intensity turn people off. Again, this is frustrating, because I'm driven by passion and determination. I've been successful as a technical expert thus far in my career, but now my career has become somewhat static. I've always been able to grasp abstract concepts quickly. Once I understand the concept and have the facts to support it, I hold tight to my conviction regarding the matter, whatever it is. Sometimes conflicts arise when the person with an opposing idea has not done their homework. Sometimes, because others have not done their homework, I get labeled as someone who is difficult to negotiate with.*

*I want to be an effective person and employee. I realize that this comes from building good relationships with people. As a matter of fact, I have several harmonious personal relationships with friends because we accept each other without needing to change or control one another. We have differing views on issues without conflict. I think that it is because we trust and believe in each other enough that we never feel like we are going to lose anything.*

*I really do not know how to have that kind of relationship with the people I work with. However, maybe there is another technique that I could use that could also be effective. Do you have any suggestions? What steps should I take to change this short-circuit that I've created in my career?*

**Response:** The problem you present must be driving you slightly batty. Your commitment to the issues on the job is something for which you deserve reward and affirmation, rather than rejection and the feeling of being ignored.

Healing existing relationships is not an easy task. However, several ideas come to mind:

1. The first is that you should explore changing your work situation: perhaps there is another company you could work for, or another division within your existing company.

2. Another possibility depends on your capacity to take time out from your career. Can you afford a year or so studying in order to enhance your marketable skills, whether within your existing company, in another firm, or in a different business?

3.  If you were to take a sabbatical, that might also give you time to catch your breath as well as give your workplace colleagues, both superiors and subordinates, an opportunity to realize what they're missing when you're not there. It could also give you a chance to explore the overall context of your professional focus, give you a chance to "chill out" and become more relaxed about the issues troubling your current workplace situation.

4.  Staying within your existing work environment will require some serious effort on your part to heal troubled relationships and enhance those relationships that are promising. Within this range of choices I would recommend that you take an interest in each individual with whom you interact.

You can't be all over them, smothering them with attention; rather, a more subtle approach should be undertaken. The first thing to do is to learn what is important to each person: The ego gratification of getting his or her name attached to a particular solution? Being taken seriously in meetings? More rewards (financial, title, other resources)? You need to be an ear rather than a mouth—one of the hardest things to do in the world.

You need to ask yourself whether you care who gets credit for what sorts of accomplishments, whether your ego makes it hard to share credit with others. Most likely, from the sound of your note, you are a person whose contributions are quite significant. The question is, how much you care about who knows the ideas are yours? When people dig in their heels—whether it's you or somebody else—they are fighting for position rather than focusing on solving the problem. When people feel they are being judged, they get defensive and thus harder to move.

I am impressed that you have concluded that you have created your career's "short-circuit." You may be overstating your culpability, but that certainly indicates a depth of character in your willingness to look at yourself and not just at others. Your self-exploration and some research about alternatives may be the most effective steps you can take. When you're up against a brick wall, there are several choices: keep banging into it to knock it down, try to take it down brick by brick, or look for a different direction to travel in.

# Am I an Unreasonable Person?

## From: Mary, Bethesda, Maryland

**Question:** *I am in a real bind and need your immediate advice! While negotiating the use of shared PC's with a peer from another department, she erupted in anger, saying that I am the most unreasonable person in the company she's had to deal with; she even threatened to walk out of the negotiations. I really want to ensure a win-win result but I need your help. What should my response be to this situation?*

**Response:** It can be quite shocking to be called unreasonable without warning; it certainly makes it more difficult for you to negotiate in a calm manner.

The first thing you should do is ask questions. Clearly it is important to examine your relationship with your angry peer to see whether there is anything in your history that might be relevant to the apparent problem. It might also make sense to ask questions of other people: How do they view you? What have they experienced in dealing with her? Does your peer have any issues that relate to a) sharing facilities, b) your department, or c) any external characteristics that you and your peer do not share (such as gender, ethnicity, role, level of seniority)?

Most importantly, you should very gently and diplomatically try to find out your peer's interests and concerns. Open-ended questions on the order of "How do you mean that?" "Why is that important?" and "Is there a better way to accomplish the objective?" may give her a chance to inform you of things about which you may have been ignorant. You need to find out whether you or a particular issue are the problem.

You should also ask yourself what kind of long-term relationship is involved or is desired. How do you and your peer fit into that scheme of things within the company and with one another? What interests do you have in the situation? Is this particular peer a necessary element of the project or this aspect of company operations in relationship to you? Are there any hierarchical issues? Are the two of you the appropriate decision-makers, or should another party be involved to make decisions or facilitate the decision-making?

There is nothing wrong with expressing feelings: "When I hear myself called unreasonable, it makes me feel insecure [or whatever]." But don't trade accusations: "When you call me names that just shows how unreasonable you are."

Information is the fundamental asset exchanged in every negotiation. Why did this occur? You learn the most with your ears open and your mouth closed.

---

## Nasty Habits, Too Close for Comfort

### From: Harry, New York City

**Question:** *I work as an analyst with this company. The person I work with sits right next to me and has a very dirty habit of picking his nose all the time. On the other side of me, there is another person who keeps humming songs all the time. I really don't know how to tell both of them, especially the one who keeps digging into his nose, that their habits are annoying and distracting (and even disgusting).*

**Response:** If the people you sit between are at the same hierarchical level as you, it may be a little less difficult than if either of them is at a superior level.

You have an interest in a comfortable workplace: it will help you be more productive. You have an interest in feeling personally comfortable and not offended by what is going on next to you: it will reduce your stress level. Simple solutions might involve changing the location of your workspace or changing the direction of your gaze. But that is not likely to solve the problem. The nose picking is indeed something that cannot be masked. The humming may be overcome if you start listening to your own portable music device, if that is allowed. You may be concerned that if you raise the issue of nose picking and humming, you'll embarrass your colleagues. It may be, however, that they have an interest in developing a comfortable work environment, too, and that could include not causing offense to their colleagues.

Frankly, the simplest approach would be to talk with each one separately, saying that they may not have noticed, but they seem to have developed habits that you can't help but notice and which bother and distract you. They may not be aware of their habits. If their reaction is hostile, it's probably time to move to a different location. If your approach is friendly and understanding, then you may be in a better position to convince them to practice their habits in private.

Ultimately, unless you are honest about your sensitivities, people will be unaware of them. If other people in the office have also noticed these habits, you may have allies who can approach the miscreants separately and ask for an improved office environment. But honesty is certainly the best policy in this situation.

---

## She Smells, but No One Will Tell Her

### From: Kit, Calgary, Canada

**Question:** *One of our coworkers here has a bad BO (body odor) problem. It would be easy if our HR department would handle it, but she is our HR department. No one seems to know how to handle this or what to say so that her feelings are not hurt. I don't believe it's an uncontrollable problem, as her hygiene leaves a lot to be desired. Can you help?*

**Response:** It is always risky to call someone's attention to a personal quality or habit that others find offensive. There are a number of steps to take.

The most straightforward one is to engage her in a private conversation, preferably away from work in a well-ventilated area. Tell her that she may not be aware of it, but when she is around, you—or "people"—notice a smell that may indicate strong body odor or perhaps clothes that need dry-cleaning. You have to keep in mind the possibility that there is an organic problem which she has no control over that makes her smell, so you have to ask whether there is a problem before saying, "You smell bad! Why don't you take a shower every morning?

Telling someone the truth, particularly when done diplomatically, is actually a way of showing respect: "If I didn't think you were a mature, sensible person, I don't know how I would deal with this subject. But since I do respect you, I feel confident that what I'm about to say won't be taken the wrong way." If you cannot see using this option, rather than launching into a frontal assault, you need to ask her a question: "People have said that when you leave a room, there is often a lingering odor or scent. Is there a health issue that causes that to happen?"

Another approach is to deal with ventilation relatively conspicuously when she enters a space—even to the point of opening windows (if your building allows that) during the winter. If open windows are not possible, turning up the ventilation system or turning on a fan that keeps her downwind from you may be a not-so-subtle hint. If she says, "I'm getting cold," you can explain that there's a smell in the room that needs to be dissipated.

If this strategy is a problem, perhaps you can find a willing customer, supplier, or other outsider who has reason to do business with your HR person. You can find out from the outsider whether they have ever noticed the BO and whether they are willing to be quoted as having told you about it.

Yet another possibility is to have an office party feature someone who sells cosmetics. Get someone whose *spiel* includes doing a makeover on one or more people. Give the salesperson a heads-up to pay special attention to the HR person as well as discussing personal hygiene habits with everyone in the room so that no one appears to be singled out. Someone selling a new line of soaps, shampoos, or perfumes may be an excellent outsider to bring the news to the person who needs to change her ways.

Honesty is certainly the best policy; it is a sign of respect and even a demonstration that "everyone is on the same team, so let's get on the same page."

It is difficult to deal with such personal issues. However, unless you get past the offensiveness the BO causes, it will always make the HR person less effective in her job because the smell will continue to overshadow all other activities in which she is involved.

---

## Everybody Is Moving, but It May Be Bad For Me

### From: Eugene, Johannesburg, South Africa

**Question:** *I am working as a consultant in the head office, but I was given an opportunity to take a new job that is a 12-hour drive away. This will be a two-year contract. I would go, but I have carved out a wonderful life here, with friends, a new girlfriend, a house and car, and so on. My girlfriend will be going to Canada soon for about 10 months (which is eating me up, too), and suddenly now I also have to move? What should I do? Should both she* *and I go away? Should I stay? Should she stay? How can I negotiate myself out of this quandary?*

**Response:** If your girlfriend's plans to visit Canada were made before you met, if her reasons for going are not (by themselves) threatening to your relationship, and if she is committed to returning to South Africa in 10 months, I would not be too worried about the risk to your relationship. Are you prepared to formalize the relationship by making plans to get married? If you have plans like that, it will be indicative to both of you of your long-term expectations. However, deciding to take a step like getting engaged just because of a planned time apart is extremely risky. Personal relationships should not be forced by outside circumstances; they need to develop on their own.

Taking the new job for two years should not be a serious problem; if you have made good friends in Johannesburg and keep in touch with them, exchange visits, and perhaps take holidays together, you should be able to maintain the relationships. In addition, from your description of your situation, you are good at making friends and should be able to make new friends during your new assignment. Perhaps your current friends know some people in the area who you will enjoy meeting.

You need to understand your own priorities: career, romantic relationship, friendships, attachments to a given locality, and distance from your family all need to be considered as you make your decisions. Throwing away an opportunity for the wrong reasons can be a mistake you might regret for a long time.

Figure out which of your interests is most important. Act on those priorities. Odds are, you will make the right choices.

---

## Negotiating With the Right Person for Salary Increases

### From: Kevin, Dubai, United Arab Emirates

**Question:** *I work in a medium-sized company. Although the owner is very wealthy, he doesn't focus on the technological elements of this high-tech business. He and his vice president call all the shots here. The vice president is* *professional, but whenever salary increments are discussed, he plays the offensive role. Some people bypass him and approach the owner directly, and receive substantial salary increases. Our top performer has not been given an increase because he didn't ask the president for it. Should he leave for better opportunity or negotiate directly with president?*

**Response:** The problem you present appears to be relatively straightforward. As I understand it, two people lead your small company. The president/owner is the money person, without impressive technical qualifications. The vice president is technologically qualified, but is not the drop-dead decision-maker over money issues. Clearly, it makes far more sense to deal directly with the president over pay issues. While the vice president may have putative responsibility, he or she does not have full authority.

I would recommend that the person you describe as your top performer travel two paths: first, it would make sense for him/her to find an alternative place to work—partly as a back-up in case the negotiation with the president does not work out satisfactorily. The other reason is to find out his/her value on the open market so that, in negotiating with the president, this top performer is well-prepared with a sense of his/her worth.

After a search of alternative jobs outside the company, then it would make sense to deal directly with the president. If the president is better able to deliver a favorable compensation package, that is the only logical route to take.

# Chapter 4

# Friends, Neighbors, and Other Strangers

---

## Good Fences Make Bad Neighbors

### From: Arnie, Sausalito, California

**Question:** *My father is being sued by his neighbor for what the neighbor says is "half" the cost of the 6-foot-tall wood fence and a 3-foot-tall retaining wall he put up (30 feet long and total height of 9 feet). There was an existing 4-foot-tall wood fence and a 3-foot-tall retaining wall, but the neighbor decided to tear that down and put up a new one. He and my father talked earlier about sharing the cost, with the condition that my father wanted to be there to negotiate the pricing with whomever does the work.*

*However, the neighbor hired day laborers without my father's consent and did the negotiating by himself. Later, the neighbor went to my dad and gave him a bill for $1,800, which he claimed is half of the total cost. My dad refused to pay him because he had no knowledge of who was being hired and how much it cost. In addition, the retaining wall the neighbor put up has no value to my dad. What it is doing is adding to the neighbor's property by enabling him to flatten out his lot.*

*Finally, the neighbor is charging my dad $18 an hour for the neighbor's efforts.*

*My question is, who is responsible for the cost of this fence and retaining wall? And what about the ridiculous charge for the neighbor's own labor?*

**Response:** It sounds as if your father is well-served by the existence of a barrier between his neighbor's property and his own. The neighbor you describe does not sound like a very honorable person. If the two men shook hands on a deal that included your father in the hiring decision, the neighbor breached that agreement. Moreover, under common law in many States, any agreement with a cash value of more than $100 must be in the form of a signed contract to be enforceable. You should check to see whether this is the case in California.

If your father feels that he has indeed benefited from the erection of the fence and/or the retaining wall, he may want to make a friendly gesture and pay for some of the costs. It depends on his long-term interests about his relationship with the neighbor. It may be that the neighbor presented an outrageous bill with the expectation that he and your father would settle on a different figure after negotiating with each other. You or your dad should explore this possibility before simply walking away from the situation—and risking long-term negative feelings across the fence.

Your father should be given the opportunity to review receipts for payments made by the neighbor for both labor and materials. Because your father never hired the neighbor to do any of the work, even the negotiating with the day laborers, there does not appear to be any justification for paying the neighbor anything.

In this situation both you and your father should consider the long-term consequences of the choices you can make. When a fence between my house and one of my neighbor's needed replacing, I paid for the whole thing because I wanted to protect my privacy with the fence, control its design, and strengthen the relationship. With another neighbor I did the exact opposite; they created a barrier between our properties which I had no involvement in designing or planning. Because it was their project, I had no reason or obligation to pay.

It sounds as if your father's neighbor is trying to take advantage of your dad. I cannot see any contractual obligation on your father's part to pay anything for this project.

# My Neighbors Are Making My Home a House of Horrors

### From: Curtis, Memphis, Tennessee

**Question:** *I live in an apartment. My neighbors are somewhat inconsiderate. Here is the scoop: I consider myself an ordinary Joe. I am your basic quiet, respectful neighbor. My neighbor found himself a girlfriend. She brought with her three children. They are noisy at times. I can deal with this.*

*My problem is that they interrupt my privacy. I like to keep to myself. They like to knock on my door often. They have no jobs. They like to ask me if I can give them money for unimportant things, like cigarettes. They have no telephone. They ask if they can use mine often. They have a dog. They like to leave him out on the balcony that overlooks an extremely busy street. The dog barks constantly. We share a small staircase. They like to leave their 55-gallon trashcan full of stinking, fly-ridden garbage there. I now have cockroaches. My trashcan has a lid and liner which I empty regularly. We have a dumpster not more than 50 yards away. These people lock their children out often while they are away or drinking.*

*What can I do?*

**Response:** The situation you describe is, indeed, terrible. Your first step should be to take a look at the options available to you: Could you move out? Is there anyone in authority regarding the maintenance of apartments (in terms of the trash problem and the dog)? Do you have other neighbors who share your feelings on any of those issues who might side with you if you complain—to the unpleasant neighbors themselves, the landlord, or even the police?

You have not indicated whether these unpleasant neighbors or their children could be threatening to you because of age differences, a tendency to violence, or simply by making things even worse by being noisier, dirtier, or more intrusive. If there have been threats of violence, are there public authorities who might be helpful? Unsupervised children are also a matter that should be of concern to public authorities. Unfortunately, all too often they are underfunded and overworked, and thus hard to depend on to take care of problems that may bother you but might seem trivial compared to other problems they face.

Once you have taken a look at your alternatives, you need to figure out what steps you can take as a matter of self-help: turn off your doorbell so the kids from next door can't bother you, use cockroach poison anywhere the critters might be able to enter your apartment, or bring a short-term guest into your own apartment who might increase your feelings of security. Having done all this, you then need to communicate clearly with your neighbors and their children. If the neighbors have serious behavioral problems, getting them to agree to be more neighborly will probably be easier than getting them to live up to their agreement.

I wonder whether their children are more civilized than the parents and whether you can form an alliance with them. For example, you might trade limited phone privileges for their maintenance of a cleaner trash bin. Perhaps you could also let the kids use the phone a certain amount if they walk the dog more often. While it doesn't sound as if you are at all interested in establishing a relationship with the kids—and it could be quite risky from a number of angles—if they see you as an ally instead of someone they can take advantage of, perhaps they will make life a bit more pleasant for you. Maybe you could help them get a key to their apartment so they're not stuck outside. But again, you need to consider whether the kids' access to their home is likely to make your life any better in the long-term.

Negotiation works best when it is symmetrical, when the negotiating parties are more or less equally motivated and able to work out an agreement. It does not sound as if there is much symmetry between you and the "adults" next door. The children may be more promising as potential negotiation partners.

On the whole it sounds as if you are facing an out-of-control situation. Escape may be the wisest answer if you can find a way to do so.

# The "Neighborhood Nazi"

## From: Aimee, Waco, Texas

**Question:** *My family and I have just moved to a new neighborhood. We are a newly married couple in our 30s and we have two children from previous relationships, ages 5 and 9.*

*We have lived in the house we are renting for almost three months. Everything has been great until just recently, when we received an anonymous letter in our mailbox calling us "white trash" and asking us to move back to the "trailer park," since renters are not wanted in the neighborhood. It was a very degrading letter and it was also completely unwarranted. It was put in all of the neighbors' mailboxes within a 10-house radius.*

*The house we live in had been abandoned for almost a year, and admittedly needs a lot of landscaping work. We spread new grass seed, trimmed the trees, edged the yard, and have taken care of it all the best we can. We are not going to fully landscape a house that isn't ours. But our next-door neighbor has been obsessed with telling us how we ought to do our yard. We are pretty sure that he is the letter writer. Before the letter he was Mr. Nice Guy; now his attitude has totally changed. He has banned our children from playing with his and has made threatening comments toward us.*

*We have reported all this behavior to the police and the postal inspector, and we went door to door and asked if anyone knew who wrote the letter, and that if they had a problem with us, to let us know. We put up pink flamingos in our front yard to make fun of whoever was making fun of us. The pink flamingos were thrown over our fence while we were out one day. We then called the police and reported it once again. The only person outside that day was the neighbor who we suspect wrote the threatening letter. He told the police he knew nothing about it. It is clear he is lying.*

*We have no idea what to do now. We all have to live in peace, and especially our children. They are now fearful of going out to play, that this one neighbor may attack them. This person is obviously the "Neighborhood Nazi" and is not going to rest until we are gone. We are not going to back down and move—after all, we just got here.*

*How can this be resolved?*

**Response:** It is appalling to hear of such inappropriate behavior by adults, but I am genuinely impressed with your sense of humor regarding the pink flamingos. That takes a lot of self-confidence and shows that you and your husband have a lot of class. Depending on your resources (space, time, money, and remaining sense of humor) it could make good sense to focus on this situation as dependent on relationships.

From the sound of things, you have made the well-being and comfort of your children a priority. If making their life good is the first issue you want to address, you want to investigate and develop what negotiators call your BATNA, or Best Alternative to a Negotiated Agreement. In this case, you should be looking for other kids for playmates for your children. Inviting other children to your house can be a good ice-breaker. It may be worthwhile to find out what activities or toys are popular in your neighborhood—and then see whether you can offer that for your kids and their guests to enjoy.

You and your husband should also work on developing relationships with other people who live close by. You may have shared interests in spectator sports, in jogging, or some other activity that is enhanced when shared with others. Perhaps you will find people with whom you can share your interests: for example, church, neighborhood beautification, traffic safety, school issues, and so on. It could make sense to find some "champions" among your neighbors, people who will treat you with respect and who might welcome an invitation to pop over for a cookout.

It is crucial not to make the nastiness the focus of your conversations or other activities. Don't position yourselves as "those people whom someone called White Trash." Unless you like the pink flamingos, now that you've demonstrated your good humor, perhaps it's time to replace them with some nice flowering plants or bushes. If it becomes known that the pink flamingos got in the way of your plans for the yard, it shows that you are contributing to the neighborhood—rather than simply getting rid of a nasty symbol.

In effect you need to negotiate your way into the community one neighbor at a time. You will certainly find people of goodwill by taking it easy and not getting rattled at small things. Of course, the letter and pink flamingos were not small things, but if you treat them as such, that is what they will become.

It could be interesting to learn more about the history of the neighborhood and the house where you live. There may be issues from the past that have created bad vibes that you walked into without any warning. Understanding more about them may also help you come up with a creative solution.

---

# She's the Self-Appointed Neighborhood Cop

### From: Brian, St. Joseph, Missouri

**Question:** *My wife and I bought our house about 6 years ago. When we got the house it needed a little modernization, which we have done. We have 3 boys, aged 18, 15, and 13. They are normal boys and don't do anything destructive at all.*

*Now to the problem. We have a neighbor two houses away who thinks that she is the neighborhood police. She calls the police, the animal control officer, and the fire department on us all the time. The boys and I like to sit out in our back yard and shoot nuisance birds (blue jays, grackles, and starlings) with our pellet gun. They do not shoot the pellet gun when my wife or I are not home.*

*The unofficial neighborhood police called the real police and made up some terrible story that the boys were out aiming the pellet gun at her windows, and that she was picking up all kinds of dead birds in her yard. I know this is not true because I am a very avid hunter, and thus I am very safety minded when it comes to any kind of gun. My kids have been brought up with a very firm understanding of gun safety and handling. If they shoot a bird, they go pick it up and put it in our trash can. The real police officer told me that he understood what was going on, and that he wasn't going to do anything until they got more calls, at which point they would have to issue me a ticket.*

*Every summer the animal control officer shows up about once or twice a month saying that they got a call that our dog, a yellow lab, has terrible living conditions. I am a union carpenter, and I was taught to always to overbuild and never underbuild. The dog kennel is a concrete slab that is 6" thick, 6 feet wide, and 12 feet long. I bought a welded dog kennel with a nice gate and it* even has a chain link top to it. This woman called me to ask if she could let my dog loose in her back yard because "the poor dog never gets any exercise." She never sees the times I take my dog duck hunting, or walking around the block at night, or just out to the river for a swim.

When I burn leaves in the fall or spring, she calls the fire department.

After the police showed up over the pellet gun deal, I went down and confronted her. She is a very rude and mean person. After a little conversation she lightened up a little, and we were able to actually talk like adults. I told her that if she had a problem, she could always come and talk to me, and that there was really no need in calling the police, dog catcher, fire department, or anyone else. Things have been pretty good for a while. We have been waving at each other from our yards or while driving by. She did call to see if I would let her have my dog in her yard.

Christmas Eve the doorbell rang, and it was the animal control officer. He said that he had gotten a call that my dog was acting sick, and didn't have good cold-weather living conditions. I had to go out with the dogcatcher to inspect my dog and its house. He hadn't been out to see us before, and commented on what a great kennel my dog had, and that it was one of the better ones he had seen in a long time.

I am so tired of this neighbor thinking that she needs to run everyone's life. She has a little yappy housedog that she lets out every three or four hours. This dog barks the whole time it is out. When the kids are at the house next door playing basketball, she will let her dog out. They holler at it to shut up, then she comes out and yells at the kids to shut up, and "don't yell at her dog." We have lived with her yappy dog and never said anything. She has a cat that comes to our yard to do its duty in our plants. This cat also gets into our trash. We live with her cat, too, and never say anything.

I am to the point of retaliation with this woman. I called the animal control office on her yappy dog the other day. I would love to use my pellet gun on her dang cat. I would love to go down there and tell her that if she wants to start a neighborhood war, she has started it with the wrong person. Can you tell me of a good plan of attack on this self-elected neighborhood official?

**Response:** When you ask for a "plan of attack" it sounds as if you are already preparing to go to war. While the situation you describe sounds unbelievably annoying, you need to give careful consideration to the most sensible way(s) to respond. First you need to ask yourself some questions:

1. Is your family the only one targeted by your unpleasant neighbor? If other neighbors have similar problems with her, it could make excellent sense to coordinate your responses. Some may have found ways to solve the problem and their advice could be helpful. On the other hand, if your family is the only one she doesn't get along with, you need to ask yourself what makes your family different from her other neighbors: children, pets, the pellet guns, or other possessions or activities that differentiate you from other people in the area. If this is the situation, you need to examine whether there are things about yourselves that you would be willing to offer to change when you are bargaining with the self-appointed policewoman to improve the situation.

2. What are your short- and long-term interests? Are you concerned about your sons feeling victimized? Does your unfriendly neighbor's harassment create stress that has a negative impact on your health, your relationships with other people, or any other part of your life? Do you want a hassle-free life in your neighborhood, or are you more concerned with punishing your annoying neighbor for the aggravation she brings you? How will your response to this neighbor affect your reputation within the neighborhood or in other parts of the community (for example, church, your work, or your kids' schools)?

The strategy you develop should reflect your interests and the interests of people who either depend on you or will be impacted by your behavior. Your strategy should also reflect your comprehension of what's making your neighbor behave so unpleasantly. If she has personal issues that predate your arrival on the scene, understanding them may help you figure out the best way to approach the situation.

Having said all that, you are probably still wondering what steps you can take. Fundamentally you need to consider your BATNA, your Best Alternative to a Negotiated Agreement. You can think of BATNA as your understanding that you have a variety of options, including just walking away. Think about the likely results if you a) ignore the neighbor, b) have a nasty confrontation, c) work out a civilized discussion, d) get other neighbors on your side, e) go to the public authorities and ask for a restraining order on her interference in your life, or take some other approach. Once you have a good sense of your BATNA, you can make a more pragmatic decision about how to go forward. Just letting off steam is not a good enough reason to go ballistic. You'll still have to live with the consequences.

Ultimately, if you approach the neighbor, remembering that you've had a peaceful period after an earlier conversation, spend more time asking questions, and listen closely to the answers, you are likely to learn what it's going to take to defuse the situation. If you have thought about the alternatives—what you can offer, what you can concede, and the same sorts of things you might hope for or expect from her—you are more likely to structure your questions and proposals in a calm, confident, and convincing way. You need to consider who in your family is likely to be the most effective spokesperson.

Above all, don't let your emotions control you. Your job is to control your emotions and use them for the best effect. Remember the rule: only one person can be angry at a time. Otherwise conflict will escalate and resolution will escape you.

---

## You're Not The Light Of My Life

### From: Darla, Perth Amboy, New Jersey

**Question:** *My neighbor has been shining a 300-watt light on my house (it is his security light). We asked him very nicely to please point the light down so it does not shine in our bedroom window. He said no, so we ended up calling the zoning officer of our town, because it is illegal to shine a light outside your property line. Now my neighbor parks his cars in front of my house out of spite and has pointed his light slightly upward again—sort of testing the limits. What should be my next step? This man is unapproachable and quick-tempered.*

**Response:** Let's take a look at this problem from the last element of your question first. You say your neighbor is quick-tempered. You should ask yourself what he might be capable of if he became really angry. There are other non-violent steps he might take in addition to parking cars in front of your house—loud music late at night, telephone calls at inconvenient hours, even "mistakenly" dumping trash onto your property. Although each of these may give you an opening for calling the zoning officer or even the police, particularly if the neighbor resorts to even more serious behavior, you need to examine whether you have a more attractive alternative to any of those possible outcomes.

At the same time, it could be worth exploring whether there are troublesome consequences to his improper behavior. For example, how would he feel if his "trespassing" were to cost him money? Although it sounds as though fighting fire with fire will only lead to escalation, perhaps he is exceeding his legal rights; perhaps a lawyer would conclude that the neighbor is attempting to grab an easement which interferes with your property rights.

I am not suggesting that you start a legal battle, but rather that before you take any steps, you explore—as creatively as possible—what kinds of outcomes either party might face from mutually negative actions. Does this neighbor have good or bad relations with other neighbors? Do any of them have experience solving problems with him?

Next, you should explore whether you and your neighbor share any interests. Does your neighborhood as a whole face any issues where you might be on the same side—for example, a stop sign needed at a particular intersection, concerns about security, or groundwater pollution? If you do have any shared interests, perhaps beginning with those may be a means for breaking the cycle of disagreement. If your neighbor is indeed concerned about security (thus the light), perhaps you should communicate with him about installing security lights on your own property that complements his light.

Your portrayal of the situation makes it sound as though the problem is entirely one-sided. Perhaps that is the case. However, conflicts that are viewed as being one-sided, where only one party is the "bad guy," offer very little leeway to the other side to bring about change. I would not suggest you beg forgiveness, but rather that you remind yourself that solving this problem by escalating the conflict will not work out favorably. Think of all the possible reasons why your neighbor might be behaving as he has—then, use those assumptions to develop a series of questions to ask him (or other people whom he'll listen too) to figure out how his issues can be resolved.

He may feel that there is some sort of security benefit from a light that's aimed high up. Ask him if he would like to raise it so that the light starts at your roofline. Ask him if a light aimed down at the space between his house and yours would also help. Does he have security lights aimed away from your house—toward other neighbors, the street, a back alley? And finally, is the problem he is trying to solve related to his security or his ego? ("Nobody tells me what to do with my property.")

Make sure that in your communication with him, you do not act as if you were his victim. That only invites more trouble. Think about the problems you share and then find ways to solve the problems in ways that don't reflect on you or him.

If you keep the worst possible outcome in mind, that will give you a context against which to test your further steps. Deliberation is important in any situation where a fast response could take you in the wrong direction.

---

## I Helped Friends Buy/Sell a Car— Am I Their Keeper?

### From: Theresa, Cleveland, Ohio

**Question:** *I have a friend who purchased a car from a coworker of mine in late January. I introduced my friend and my coworker to one another and within a week or two the car was sold.*

*It is now August and, unbeknownst to me, my friend never had the title transferred into his name. In the seven months that my friend has had the car, he has acquired two parking tickets. My coworker was recently pulled over for running a red light and had to go through great lengths to prove the car and the tickets did not belong to him. My coworker has placed numerous calls to my friend's home and threatened to have the car reported stolen if my friend does not have the title transferred and the old plates returned to my coworker. My friend thinks my coworker is out of line by calling his home and harassing his family because he thinks it is none of their business. My friend refuses to call my coworker back and let him know when he plans on taking care of changing the title.*

*My friend refuses to take responsibility. My friend doesn't seem to realize that he is the one who is going to lose in a big way if he sits around and does nothing to remedy the situation. I have talked to him about this, but it seems that all I have done is "preach" about it. I would like some hints or suggestions how to negotiate a solution or present it to him in a different way that does not appear as though I am telling him what to do. Please help!*

**Response:** Your story is yet another example of the risks one takes arranging business transactions between friends and/or colleagues. When you introduced your friend to your coworker, you probably had no idea the car would change hands. If that is the case, you shouldn't feel embarrassed or responsible. If you brought them together in order to get the car sold, however, then you have good reason to feel some degree of responsibility. Your friend is exhibiting incredible irresponsibility. He is causing your coworker grief and, in doing so, creating problems for you.

From the sounds of things, neither party has behaved in a businesslike manner in the sale of the car. The seller should not have let the car leave his possession without having transferred the title and the plates to the buyer. And the buyer was irresponsible in not bothering to fulfill his legal obligation to make sure that he had the plates and title when the car changed hands. However, your description of the situation makes it sound as though the buyer was more irresponsible than the seller.

Your top interest revolves around your relationship with both of these people; what you need to do is determine which relationship is more important. You should also assess, as best you can, how important their relationship with you is to them. If your friend needs you more than you need him, then you may have the capacity to influence his behavior. If that is not the case, however, your capacity to influence him is minimal, in which case you and the coworker need to have an honest talk about your role in this situation.

You may be able to help your coworker get out from under this situation if you can discover any interests your friend may have in cleaning up his act. Perhaps you can do a better job of research on this issue than your coworker can. Unless there is some way to motivate your friend to behave as an adult, I agree with him that all you are doing is "preaching" to him—and his use of that phrase makes it clear that he is not a believing member of your "congregation."

Barring some breakthrough in learning about interests that will motivate the friend to complete the transaction properly, I'm afraid your coworker's best alternative (BATNA) is to look for legal avenues to get the problem solved.

---

# It's a Close Community—
# Perhaps Too Close

### From: Charlene, Chula Vista, California

**Question:** *I'm not sure how to phrase my question without sounding arrogant, but here goes. I am a strong Christian leader in our church, school, and community. My husband and I are self-made multimillionaires at age 45 through investments in many properties. We both came from very humble backgrounds. We have worked very hard to get ahead in life. We help many people in need as we feel that God has really blessed us and we need to be good stewards with his money. I do not discuss our financial status with others, although it is pretty obvious because word gets out when you are a donor.*

*My problem is how to deal with six or seven certain people who are lashing out at my children, my husband, and myself. I know it is out of jealousy, but I need to deal with these people in church, school, wherever. They are spreading untruths, sarcasm, and rude comments; they seem to just want to "X" us out of the school, church, and community.*

*We live in a small community where word travels fast. We left the school after five years because of this and put our children in a private Christian school. We are now thinking of leaving our church after nine years of active membership. I know people can be rude wherever you go, but you can only take so much of jealousy, gossiping, and rudeness. Please give me some advice.*

**Response:** People negotiate to bring about changes that favor their interests—whether in business, community life, or as consumers. It sounds as if your big interest is to be able to contribute to your community—by your actions and by giving—without suffering from nasty words directed at you or other members of your family. What could be simpler than that? However, the people you find troublesome must have something driving their actions and words. In order to figure out how to cope with the unpleasantness you face, you need to figure out what interests may underlie the rudeness of the people who are troubling you. Jealousy is not an interest; it is an emotion.

The question is, what do these people hope to gain, and how will being troublesome to you and your family bring them what they want? If they make you unhappy or uncomfortable, what "goodies" do they get? Are they trying to shore up vulnerable egos? Do they want recognition from others that they feel is going to you instead of them? Instead of being justified by faith, are they pursuing the kind of power bullies use to justify their existence? Bullies are afraid of looking weak; they are afraid of failure. Are your nemeses afraid they have failed compared to you? As you develop your assumptions about what is driving them, what you are also doing is creating a list of questions to ask them and people who know them in order to figure out whether there are ways you can help them achieve their interests in ways that don't hurt you.

From what you wrote, it sounds as though you can identify the specific individuals who are most troublesome. Can you rank them according to the difficulty you think you would have in engaging in conversation with them? Strategize by asking yourself whom you should approach first. If Mr. W or Mrs. T can be mollified/civilized, what impact will that have on other members of the "gang of 6 or 7"?

Figure out what kind of information you need from them to give you fuel for developing a peace settlement. That will tell you what questions you need to ask. Don't ask judgmental questions such as, "Why are you so lousy to me/my family?" Rather, you should try to find out whether your initial assumptions about their motivation and/or interest are accurate. Perhaps you will be surprised. Obviously, that could be either good news or bad news, but it will mean you learn something you didn't know before. If you ask open-ended questions, listening carefully to their answers will help you develop ideas that may address their interests *and* your own. That is a major first step toward reconciliation.

It may be that you simply cannot talk directly with any of them. If that's the case, can you think of anyone else whom both of you respect and who would be willing to intervene? In effect you'd be looking for someone to act as a mediator so that each side can negotiate without the stress of going face-to-face. Given the centrality of your church in your life—and perhaps that of your rude neighbors—it could be that a member of the clergy would be the most effective person to choose as a mediator. Most likely your pastor has strong interests in a peaceful congregation and, more crassly, keeping you and your husband as active members. So:

- Examine your interests, the deepest motivations that drive your decisions.

- Make educated assumptions about the interests of the troublemakers.

- Consider the alternatives available to you (what negotiators call BATNA—the Best Alternative to a Negotiated Agreement).

- Figure out whether you are better off communicating directly with the troublemakers or using an indirect route, such as mediation.

- Ask open-ended questions (either directly or through the mediator) to find out whether your assumptions are accurate.

- Look for ways to respond to their interests as well as your own in your pursuit of peace.

---

## The Sounds They Make Embarrass Us

### From: Jennie, San Diego, California

**Question:** *We have always had a certain tolerance for our upstairs neighbor's dogs barking, but recently we've been disturbed by sounds of her having sex at various hours. We live in an apartment building and the noise travels.*

*She has been a decent neighbor for the past six years, which is why we've tolerated the dogs, but the noises she and her boyfriend make are too much: They literally wake us up late at night and early in the morning. Is there any way to politely tell her that we can hear everything? It's fairly embarrassing.*

**Response:** If you have a good relationship with your neighbor, being honest in a diplomatic way is likely to be the best approach.

Remember that you are doing her a favor. Unless she is an exhibitionist, I cannot imagine she is likely to take any pleasure in learning that her romantic activities are being broadcast beyond the walls of her apartment. Viewing the situation from that angle means you are no longer complaining about noise interfering with your sleep, but rather offering her an opportunity to protect her privacy.

You should plan ahead before talking with her. Consider your BATNA, Best Alternative to a Negotiated Agreement. In the worst case scenario, can you do anything to your apartment's walls, ceiling, and/or floor to deaden outside noise? Is there anything she and her boyfriend might do that would increase your discomfort? How can you deal with the possibility they will ratchet up the unpleasantness?

You might also want to do some research on building codes in your community. It may well be that noise transmission within residential buildings is supposed to be kept within certain limits. It might cost you money, but you may want to measure the actual decibels of the barking and the romantic encounters. Some noise abatement codes prescribe noise limits based on the time of day or night. It could actually be the responsibility of your landlord to make sure the building's structure meets code requirements. Should this be the case, you need not tell your landlord the embarrassing details—just talk about sounds carrying through the walls.

---

## Our Neighbor's Shed Has Invaded Our Land

### From: Kris, Kokomo, Indiana

**Question:** *We recently purchased a new home. Because we wanted to install a fence, we had a stake survey completed. The results of the survey indicated that our neighbor's shed (which is quite elaborate, yet does not have a cement foundation) extends about two and half feet onto our property. We feel the fence definitely needs to be on or near the property line, so we would prefer they move their shed, which is within our legal rights. However, we wish to remain friendly with our neighbors, so we do not want to approach them the wrong way or seem like jerky neighbors. How should we go about approaching this problem with them and convincing them that moving their shed is a good idea? Any suggestions?*

**Response:** If your relationship with your neighbor is friendly or at least polite, there is no reason not to tell them about your plans to erect a fence. You should tell them that you had a survey done to make sure you don't put the fence on anyone else's property. Tell them you were surprised to discover their shed is partially on your property. You might suggest there are a number of possible solutions:

- They may want to have their own survey done to confirm (or yield a dispute with) the findings of your survey. You can then ask them to move their shed.

- If they don't want to move the shed at their own expense, you need to consider whether financial or other kind of help from you will help get the shed moved.

- If moving the shed creates real problems, you might want to consider trading the land their shed occupies to them in exchange for land from them. Perhaps they would want to buy the portion of your land their shed occupies.

If you feel it's likely that they will become confrontational, you need to examine your interests very carefully before you talk with them. What is more important—a good neighborly relationship, getting rid of the shed's intrusion on your property, or something else? Do you have a good BATNA (Best Alternative to a Negotiated Agreement)? For example, could you simply move the shed yourselves? Could you erect a fence that cuts through or climbs over the shed? Can you rely on any public authorities to come to your aid? What will your relationship with these neighbors do to your reputation in the neighborhood? How will each of the different possible outcomes impact the level of stress in your life?

Once you have considered these issues, try to find out how much your neighbors value their relationship with you. If they really care about that, it may increase your capacity to influence them to cooperate.

---

# When I Keep Score, My Friends Aren't Friendly

### From: Mary, Boca Raton, Florida

**Question:** *I want to be nice. However, when my group gets together to play cards, I am usually the scorekeeper. It really bothers me when they check my arithmetic. I resent their looking over my shoulder. I have offered to give the score-keeping job to someone else, but invariably I wind up doing it. The amount of money we play for is less than two dollars. How can I keep score and still keep my cool when my score-keeping is constantly under a microscope? These people are my friends. I don't want to make a fuss in any way.*

**Response:** Perhaps saying you want to be nice is really a way of saying "I haven't got the nerve to be honest with my friends."

The real issue is that some people derive pleasure or some other kind of reward from controversy, even when the stakes are low. You face the difficult job of dealing with disagreement without being disagreeable and without escalating possible conflict.

It doesn't sound as though you're gaining anything from acting as scorekeeper. If you refuse to accept the job and your friends counter by saying, "No one else can do it," you should say, "I will do it on one condition: no quibbling with my job performance. If my score-keeping is questioned, I will not do it again." And then, keep your word.

Of course, you can always think of how miserable the troublemakers would be if you deprived them of a chance to be a pain. If you look at it that way, you'll realize just how much you've been contributing to your friends' daily pleasure in life. You're actually doing them a favor! Just remember that they've chosen the nicest person available to pick on because they know that choosing the wrong target could backfire on them. You are doing a public service. Pat yourself on the back and enjoy.

---

## First He Was My Friend, Now He's My Business Partner—And It's Not Working

### From: Jeff, Marlton, New Jersey

**Question:** *My partner and I started a corporation only six months ago and already it is clear that we will not be able to go on as partners. We have extremely different work ethics and values. We have been friends for years before this and we had big plans. However, I don't believe that I will be able to continue working with him. We borrowed some money from my parents and received a smaller loan from the bank. I want to continue with the company; I just want him out. What should I do?*

**Response:** Developing business relationships with friends can be extraordinarily risky, whereas becoming friendly with people you already know at work is probably less likely to cause difficulties. The challenge with friends is that you are changing the nature of the relationship.

You and your partner need to communicate clearly with each other. In order to do this you need to do a good deal of homework ahead of time. Figure out who are stakeholders in the situation and what their interests are. For example, your parents would probably like to be paid back. You need to assess whether you want to end the business partnership itself, and what you're prepared to accept as a consequence in terms of your personal friendship. How do you think your partner feels about this? What does he have at stake in the business relationship—and the friendship? Make a whole range of assumptions about what's important to him and to other stakeholders, and why those things are important.

Once you've made those assumptions, the next step is to undertake a reality check on the accuracy of those assumptions. Ask questions that allow for open-ended (not yes-or-no) answers so that you can learn from your partner (and any other interested parties) what is likely to convince them to reach agreement with you. Perhaps your partner would be thrilled to be bought out. If you have the money, are convinced the business can afford the investment, or can arrange a satisfactory long-term payout, this may offer the chance for a clean break. Listen for what is likely to trigger your partner's enthusiasm for splitting up. Find out how committed he is to the business. Can the business itself be split into two different organizations? And would each partner be happy going into a different aspect of the business?

Negotiation is about trading information—even when it is "only" information about the commodity about which the parties are bargaining. To trade information, you need to know what you know and what you need to know. Preparing makes that possible, and asking questions, particularly of your partner, should give you some ideas about how to move toward your objectives.

# My (Ex-friend) Partner Split and Took Our Business

### From: Jason, Chattanooga, Tennessee

**Question:** *I formed a partnership with a friend (first mistake, I know, but too late now) basically advertising products for companies through several avenues.*

*We got this idea from my partner's brother, who was already in the business doing the same thing. We got into the business and it was very similar to his brother's business in that we were advertising similar products, but as the business grew, we branched out to varied products while his brother still focused on this one type of product.*

*Things really went well. We found a company with products no one else was advertising, so we started advertising these products and ended up doing very well with them, as we were the only company advertising their products. After a year of doing great my partner calls me and states he is going to split from me and join his brother because his brother is going to start branching out with more products to advertise, he is much better at it, will be more stable, have longevity, and be more profitable.*

*So my partner left me with all the business at no charge, just a clean break, and we settled any payment from that day back. Well, within weeks of the split and as soon as they got their business up and running, they immediately started advertising the same products my old partner and I had found that no one else was advertising, competing directly against me in the same advertising avenues, which of course drove up costs and split sales in half for me.*

*So my question is, is what he is doing really ethical? Taking a marketing plan for these products no one else was advertising for and advertising them with his new partner? I can see if another competitor started advertising these products, but what about an ex-partner who takes your ideas from your partnership and uses them with his new partnership?*

**Response:** Your partner's behavior is quite unethical. However, in addition to making the mistake of going into business with a friend, you also made two others:

1.  You should have created a partnership agreement, which included an agreement that in the event of a termination of the partnership, neither partner would compete with the other for a specified period of time.

2.  When your partner announced his decision to leave the partnership, you should have tried to get a non-compete agreement from him. If he offered to settle any outstanding financial issues with you, you should have been willing to trade a non-compete agreement for some or all of the money he owed you.

You have learned an enormously expensive lesson. Ronald Reagan is credited with the expression, "Trust, but verify." In your future business dealings, don't assume potential partners, clients, or suppliers are out to cheat you. But don't depend on words when a document is more likely to provide the protection you need.

# Chapter 5

# Whose Money Is It Anyway?
# Spending Habits, Credit, and Debt

---

## How to Convince My Credit Card
## Company to Let Me off the Hook

### From: Don, Methuen, Massachusetts

**Question:** *How do I negotiate with a credit card company if I want them to accept less than the full amount I owe as full payment of the balance on my account?*

**Response:** While it is reasonably easy to understand your interest in convincing the credit card company to accept less than the full amount you owe as full payment, it is considerably more difficult to understand what interest they would have in agreeing to that. What does the credit card company stand to gain from accepting a reduced payment? Is your contract with them different from the standard contract (which normally doesn't give you any options to negotiate the amount due)?

Unless the credit card company has something to gain by letting you pay less than you owe, your attempt to change their mind is going to fail. By using the card, you agreed to their terms and created a legal liability for yourself. If they allow you to reduce your debt in the way you suggest, they will be opening themselves up to an untold number of similar attempts by other cardholders.

A far more realistic approach is to negotiate the terms of your repayment. Stop using the card and reach an agreement to pay predetermined amounts on a regular basis. Even if you go to a debt consolidation service, take out a home-equity loan, or find some other source of funds, your legal obligation for your existing debt will not disappear. According to one expert I contacted, it is possible to walk away from credit card debt under U.S. law. Filing for Chapter 7 bankruptcy will totally eliminate all unsecured credit card bills. You should consider whether this is a favorable long-term approach for you.

One of the rules of negotiating is to choose to negotiate when there is a reasonable chance that the parties each have something to gain by changing the existing situation. Unless the credit card company has something to gain, the likelihood of your being able to change the situation is effectively nil. You can change your own behavior far more readily than you can expect the credit card company's behavior to change.

---

## Earnestly Seeking Relief

### From: Eddie, Bowie, Maryland

**Question:** *I'm having financial problems, and I need to negotiate positive settlements with my creditors to avoid personal bankruptcy. What are the key factors in this type of negotiation?*

**Response:** Your creditors have one very obvious series of interests: collecting the money that is owed to them.

What you need to do is find out, creditor by creditor, whether there are any peculiar aspects of their interests in collecting that money. Are some creditors in a bigger rush? Do any of the creditors have any interest in maintaining a long-term relationship with you? Are any creditors concerned about their reputation with other borrowers—for example, borrowers in the same business or neighborhood or those that share other characteristics with you? Does any creditor have an interest in keeping you financially "alive" for personal or business reasons?

Fundamentally, your biggest job is to ask questions and listen very carefully to your creditors, seeing whether there are interests they share with you, whether there are openings for potential agreements. It is important to talk with each creditor independently; if they start acting as a group, your capacity to influence them will be reduced enormously.

In addition, your creditors need to realize that in bankruptcy, creditors tend to recover pennies on the dollar. If you can encourage them to conclude that they'll collect a larger proportion of the amount owing if you don't go through bankruptcy, that is certainly in their interest. Don't forget, however, that you cannot cut separate deals if a bankruptcy is looming. That is against the law, and such agreements are voided by the process.

Here are some positive offers you can make: time extensions, guarantees of future business once you're on your feet, payment schedules based on your income (the more you make, the more they collect), and non-financial benefits, such as being willing to stand in line for them to buy tickets to a nearly sold-out performance, offering them introductions to the best garage mechanic in town, and so on. In one case I mediated, the debtor agreed to let his lender use the debtor's vacation house four weeks a year rent-free (during an agreed-upon portion of the year). It didn't cost the debtor any money, but gave the creditor an ego boost as well as a nice place to go for vacation.

In other words, you need to be attentive, curious, and creative.

An additional possibility is to find out what your creditors think you should be interested in: reputation, creditworthiness, preserving your relationships, being able to focus on your work, keeping certain assets, and so on. When you know what they think you're willing to trade, that may also open doors to agreement.

---

## I Pay for Household Expenses, but My Husband Doesn't Contribute

### From: Diana, Kolkata, India

**Question:** *I am a working woman and I often find that my financial independence is a threat to the male dominance in this culture. Also, it is usually taken for granted that because I am financially independent, household* *expenditures will naturally be borne by me until the last amount of my income is dispensed with. Even though I have tried to plan, organize, and work out a schedule for income and expenditures and communicate this at home, it does not help. (The discussion always ends with "Let us be considerate; we will do my way.") Could you please tell me how to handle this situation, as I feel that in a family everything needs to be shared, whether it is work, income, expenses, happiness, or sadness.*

**Response:** Rather than approaching your husband with a well-organized, rationally justifiable approach, it could make sense to take the following steps:

1.  Think about the interests of the people who have something to derive from the outcome of your joint decision: you, your husband, your children, relatives on both sides, and so on. For example, if you have relatives who might become ill or otherwise dependent, whose resources will be used to assist them? If you have nothing left from your earnings, does that mean your husband is prepared to come forward with financial help if needed? If he is not prepared to be helpful under such circumstances, what will that do to his image among his friends and colleagues?

2.  Think of similar scenarios that may also reflect the interests of the individuals who have a stake in the outcome of your discussion with your husband—for example, children's education, major household expenditures (repairs, redecorating), and so on. Once you have outlined the interests of the various stakeholders, that gives you a list of questions to ask in order to learn which concerns are most likely to catch your husband's attention. When you ask him questions, they should not be designed to be answered with just a yes or a no; the questions should invite him to answer with more expansive information.

3.  Listen carefully to his answers. If he gives an answer you don't like, just sit there silently, revealing nothing with your facial expression. The power of silence is extraordinary. It is far more likely to make a person think than a swift, emotional reaction. In his answers, try to find elements you can use in your response that demonstrate you take him seriously: "I have listened to you, now it's your turn to listen to me."

4.   As you prepare, you need to think of what bargaining chips are available to you. For example, if you accept household-expense responsibility, what will he contribute to assets that will be available to you when you cease employment? Are there tax advantages to or penalties for having separate assets for a wife and her husband? In some countries, death duties are almost confiscatory, it all goes to taxes when there's no will, so it can pay to place assets in a spouse's name to avoid those taxes.

You need to ask a lot of questions to find ways to open doors to a mutually agreeable solution. You also need to determine how far you are prepared to go in responding to his one-sided approach. When someone says, "We'll do it *my* way!" that leads to a failed negotiation. Unless both parties are fully in agreement, the results may not be good over the long term. When someone can only see things his way, he could be said to be acting carrying on as a bully. Bullies are afraid of failure, so if you say, "I'm afraid we may fail to reach a real agreement," you are threatening failure, and that may be an effective wake-up call.

---

## How Can We Convince Them We're Not Leg-breakers?

### From: Michelle, Portland, Oregon

**Question:** *How do you suggest training negotiation skills to new bill collectors? I work for a bank and currently train all the new hires and I sometimes find it difficult to train negotiation skills. People have this idea that debt collection is the old-time breaking of the kneecaps. Collection in this day and age and at this bank is about helping the customer resolve their issues and providing education. Yet I struggle on how to help them negotiate for payments.*

**Response:** It may well be that the best approach to providing negotiation training for your bank's collectors is to hire an external negotiation skills training organization.

The best way to provide training in negotiation skills—as well as in other "soft" skills—is to focus on the philosophical approach you want your colleagues to use, to study that approach, and then to look for the best teaching methods for the relevant audience. When your bank's collectors are dealing with people who owe money, the collectors need to ask a lot of questions to find out what will enable people to pay their debts, what will motivate them, and what creates the risk of an adversarial relationship. Thus it could make sense for you to look at the various tools your collectors can use to develop and ask good questions, and then process the information they receive in a way that yields mutually acceptable agreements that resolve the issues and provide the education to the consumer. A one-sided resolution won't work; the party that feels they got the short end of the stick will do their best to avoid fulfilling their part of the agreement. In those cases, the negotiation has failed.

## He'd Rather Spend Us Into Bankruptcy

### From: Charlene, Naperville, Illinois

**Question:** *My husband has made really bad financial decisions in the past, which has put us in a (I would say) moderate level of debt. He has mentioned bankruptcy three times now within three months. I have been totally against this in all three conversations. I have even looked through our bills and, with his income (which is all we have right now), made a plan that could help get us out of debt by bringing our late car payments and utility bills current. Although it would be a little tight, in two months we could go back to a comfortable level of paying off our debts. In other words, we would still have bills, but nothing would be "late."*

*At first he said he would work with my plan, but the next day he went spending money the way he wanted to. He equates the small, interest-incurring bills (car and utility payments) with trying to pay just a little bit to everyone and making our car and utility payments late. He has said my plan isn't possible and would rather go for a personal bankruptcy (because I am not filing bankruptcy) and ruin his/our credit. I challenged him to go to a financial counselor to see if my plan was possible. He just keeps saying it is his debt and it doesn't affect me, and the bankruptcy won't affect me either. He does not understand my concern of future bad credit, which will cause problems when we start looking for a home. I also don't think we even need to think about bankruptcy because we are not that far into debt; we are just late on payments, and it's stressing him out!*

*He is really bad with looking at the short-term effects of things and doesn't think even two months ahead of himself. It's really making me frustrated because I don't understand why he doesn't listen to me in this situation and why my opinions have no power. Please help! Tell me how to handle this or tell me if I should just give up the fight and let him file his bankruptcy disaster.*

**Response:** Unless you are in a position to be treated as a completely separate person from a financial standpoint, it is not his "bankruptcy disaster"; it is yours, as well. You need to examine your relationship with your husband and figure out whether his failure to take your financial concerns seriously is a stand-alone issue or symptomatic of a deeper problem. By a deeper problem, I am referring to a number of possibilities: his incapacity to face reality, a lack of respect for your interests, a lack of comprehension of the long-term consequences of his approach to money, and other possibilities.

What are the possible consequences of the various courses of action that he may take, that you may take, and that the two of you may take together? Are you better off if one set of results occurs or are all the possibilities equally okay—or awful—in your mind? Moreover, if you have children, friends, or family who might be impacted in any way by bankruptcy or some other change in your situation, they, too, are stakeholders whose interests must be considered.

It is impossible to tell from your question how long you've been married or any other information relevant to your relationship. But you have the obligation to yourself, to your husband, and to the two of you as a couple to explore the impact of any course of action on how life will be in the long term. Is your husband's approach to debt parallel to alcoholism or other addictions? Are there resources in your community you can turn to for support, even if your husband is in denial? If your husband is truly addicted to unwise financial decisions, you must examine your own role as an enabler, or as a spouse who has to deal with someone with a psychological problem. If that is the situation, you are not going to solve the problem by negotiating with your husband. Unless he has a higher interest (for example, his love of you) that will override his financial peccadilloes, there's virtually nothing you can do to change his behavior.

If possible, establish your own independent financial life. Have a separate bank account, separate credit cards, and so on. Gain some degree of control over your own financial identity. That way, your credit will not be affected by your husband's. In addition to establishing separate assets, you should consult a lawyer for advice on how to protect your assets from your husband's potential failure. If you can get a job and control how your income is spent, this will offer you independence and the breathing room to make decisions for yourself, rather than feeling that every decision you make reflects on the two of you.

There is nothing stopping you from seeing a financial counselor yourself. The advice they offer may help you make wiser decisions, too.

---

## We Argue About The Way My Husband Spends Money

### From: Maggie, Saginaw, Michigan

**Question:** *I'm a college student, a stay-at-home mom, and a nurse to my epileptic husband. Please tell me how to negotiate to achieve fairness in how we share money. We fight constantly about financial issues. Although his business is not doing well, he still buys lunch for himself, his partner (his brother), and the one employee they still have left. Is this fair?*

**Response:** Arguments about money are very often really arguments about other issues; money is the symbol for underlying matters. You should take a very careful look at the interests that underlie your concerns and those of your husband. Interests are the real reasons that drive decision-making.

Ask yourself whether your concern about how money is handled happens to reflect on how appreciated you feel as a mom and as your husband's caregiver. Similarly, ask yourself whether your husband's responses and behavior reflect any ego issues he may have due to his business problems, his health, or even his relationships with his brother/partner and their employee.

Think hard about what outcomes would give you the most satisfaction and why they would please you. Perform the same kind of analysis on what your husband's preferred outcomes might be and why those would be more appealing to him than whatever alternatives might be available. All of this questioning should help you figure out what issues should be raised in your discussions, and how the underlying interests can be used to help you and your husband formulate creative ways to reach agreement. Your preparatory homework will not only help you develop a strategy; it will also tell you what assumptions you have made so you can ask questions to run reality checks on the accuracy of those assumptions.

Your husband's own answers to these questions are far more likely to help him convince himself than your suggestions—or demands.

# Chapter 6

# Negotiating Purchases, Sales, and Services

---

## They Want More Than They Paid For

### From: Oleg, Bucharest, Romania

**Question:** *We are a market consultancy company and our activity is project-based. Once a project is commissioned by a client, we send an invoice for the agreed-upon fee. We are very service-oriented, and client relationships are essential in our business.*

*The issue that I need some advice on is that recently, one of my clients requested much more involvement from me. Specifically, he asked me to do some of his internal reports, although he already has all the information to do this, and, as far as I am concerned, the project for which we charged a specific fee was concluded.*

*How would you advise me to respond to such requests without jeopardizing the relationship?*

**Response:** The first thing you have to realize is that in a service business, you always have to give the client more value than they pay for. However, there must be limits to how much you give away.

If there is a written description of the project for which your firm was hired, it is perfectly reasonable to ask your client where the extra work he is demanding is outlined in the written agreement—but don't ask this question unless you know the answer in advance. If there is no written agreement, or if there is a chance you will have a difference of opinion that could lead to conflict, you have to take steps to correct the situation before it gets out of control.

When your client makes new demands, you need to ask how they are relevant to the original project. Your question should not give the client the opportunity to say, "Yes, it is relevant, now go do the work." Rather, your question should give the client a chance to try to sell you on what he wants. If you do the extra work, will it jeopardize your capacity to deliver the project within the allotted time period?

The next step is to take notes and create a document that describes the project. Both parties should sign that document. You can make it clear to the client that you want to do an excellent job and that you and he need to agree on benchmarks to measure your accomplishments. Any changes thereafter will cost more money.

It is crucial to tell your client that you do indeed value the relationship. You also need to say that you have an obligation to your own company to contribute to its profitability and not to create a money-losing situation. If you have partners or other colleagues in your consultancy, you can tell your client that doing the extra work "this time" could jeopardize your partners', colleagues', or owner's interest in future work with him.

The problem you describe sounds as if the client's personality is the central issue. You should think of other issues that may not relate to his personality, such as your time, other resources of his company or yours, project deadlines, and so on. Focus on the substantive issues; don't make it personal. You should make the issue of the relationship personal; talk about your feelings, ask about his.

This may not solve everything, but it may give you enough to think about to develop a strategy specific to this problem.

---

# The Builders Won't Cooperate

## From: Bud, Salisbury, Maryland

**Question:** *I plan to build a new home and fund it through a construction loan. I'm having trouble negotiating with the builders because they increase their prices just before we are ready to sign a contract. In two cases we walked away because they would not change their price back, and now one builder is suing us for plans and surveys for which we have no use (the house was not affordable and did not fit on our lot). It's like the builders always have a win-win outcome.*

**Response:** The last line of your question needs a bit of clarification; a win-win outcome means that each of the negotiating parties feels that he/she has achieved his/her objectives. I suspect that the point you were trying to make is that builders always win, to the detriment of their customers.

The attempt of one of the builders to sue you may or may not need to be taken seriously. If you signed any sort of agreement with that builder, the agreement can be the basis of legal action. On the other hand, if your deal with that builder was simply a matter of conversation, generally speaking, under common law in the United States, no agreement with a price/value of 100 dollars or more can be enforced at law without a written contract. I do not have any idea whether this is the case where you are.

Clearly, as you explore the possibilities for getting your house built, you need to have a good idea of the size, price, and other limits before you undertake any further discussions with builders. Ask neighbors, other people you know, and your lender if they have any suggestions to make regarding builders; who is worth meeting, and who might be a problem.

As of this writing, in many areas of the country, housing construction is a seller's market; the builders have more business than they need. Things always change, so perhaps you should view timing as an issue in your planning. Or it may be that you should look for builders from nearby localities or states where business is not quite as good. They may do a fine job for a better price. Ultimately, the balance of power in the negotiation process needs to be measured all the time; knowing what alternatives are available helps the balance of power become more favorable for you.

---

# What Can I Negotiate When I Buy a Home or Arrange a Mortgage?

### From: Debbie, Ontario, Canada

**Question:** *I'm buying my first house. What items can I negotiate for with the bank and/or mortgage company as well as the sellers of the house?*

**Response:** There are different items to negotiate when you are dealing with the bank or mortgage company and when you are dealing with the sellers of the house.

In purchasing a house—and borrowing the money to pay for it—you should think of *all* items as negotiable. After all, you have to live with the consequences as long as you own the house. Thus, it is fully appropriate to raise any issue you consider important. It is no less important to do so respectfully and with tact. The lending institution may have strict rules, but they also have competition. Have your lawyer tell you about relevant local laws relating to home mortgages as well as home purchases. In fact, you should also make sure you are represented by a lawyer who is routinely involved with home sales; a tax lawyer or personal injury lawyer will probably not be able to give you the advice you need.

With the lending institution, the issues most likely to be the subject of negotiation are amount of mortgage, length of term, whether or not the interest rate is adjustable, the interest rate itself, whether you have to pay the up-front fees (generally called *points*), who pays for the lawyer—in other words, virtually every element of the agreement. And just as an example, I recommend that you *not* use the lending institution's lawyer to represent you. The lender has interests that may be in conflict with your own, so you have to be careful in this area.

In terms of negotiating with the seller, a lot depends on local customs. In some countries, houses are sold stripped to the walls: no appliances, carpeting, or hardware. So you need to find out what is normally included in a house sale.

The most important thing to do in advance of purchasing a house is to have it inspected by a reputable, preferably certified, home inspector. The inspector should tell you whether the house is in conformity with all codes and whether any elements need repair. If a seller won't agree to an inspection, you may want to reconsider your interest in buying that particular house.

Some of the other items that may be worth discussing include transfer of warranties on appliances remaining in the house, repairs to the roof or other parts of the house that need fixing, ownership transfer date, and adjustment of the price based on problems found by the home inspector.

One other thing to remember: owning a house is an expensive proposition. Although the largest chunk of money may go to actually purchasing the property, upkeep, taxes, furnishing, and decorating will always present you with opportunities to spend money.

---

## They're in the Driver's Seat and They're Driving Me Crazy

### From: Thurman, Atlanta, Georgia

**Question:** *I am purchasing a new home in a new subdivision in the Atlanta area. What I am finding is that new homes are selling so quickly that the builders are not very accommodating. What can I do to increase my negotiating leverage when I sit down during the contract negotiations (especially with production builders)?*

**Response:** The greater your commitment to buying your new house in a particular area, the greater the imbalance of power between you and the seller of the housing you are thinking of buying.

You need to consider your BATNA, your Best Alternative to a Negotiated Agreement. Are there other locations where the available housing is more favorably priced? If you are committed to a particular location, perhaps the best way to strengthen your BATNA does not relate to what the builders may have to offer, but rather such issues as financing alternatives or other creative ways to make the monthly cost more attractive.

Sometimes the issues that arise in the purchase of a new house relate to the "accessories": decor, trim, interior or exterior surfaces, landscaping, irrigation, and/or other structural factors. Of course you also need to consider such issues as access to recreational facilities, school quality (and distance), taxes, and insurance cost variables.

When you are faced with another party who has no particular need for an agreement with you, it's important to find out whether there are any areas that are open for negotiation that will improve the ultimate agreement. If there is a total imbalance—if they have what you want and there's nothing you can offer to modify their demands—you need to decide just how badly you want what they're selling. Unless you have an alternative, you should look for ways to reduce the pain. If you are going to end up with a house you really want, that may be the ultimate measure of the value of the transaction to you. You need to be honest with yourself about your priorities and then act accordingly.

---

## Bargaining to Buy a New Home

### From: Tanya, Bellflower, California

**Question:** *I am interested in purchasing a new townhome in California. I have been looking for quite some time and I have noticed that the bargaining power for the buyer seems to be associated with the location. The farther the property is from Los Angeles, the more the builder/seller is willing to negotiate. I did speak with the builder about their incentives, and they told me that due to the fact that the buildings are selling, the incentives they offer are (in my view) nominal at best. However, all around the area, there are tons are homes for sale. How should I approach this?*

**Response:** The incentives offered upfront by the developer are not binding on you. You should certainly accept whatever incentives the developer offers that happen to meet your interests, but you should not stop at that point and accept the whole deal. The incentives a seller builds into her offer are what the seller has already factored in to her preferred deal. Negotiation is about trading things of value; if the developer is prepared to give things away (in the form of incentives) if you just ask for them, she is not bargaining away anything that was not already on the table—in her mind, at least.

Before taking your next steps, you should do your homework about your housing choices. Are there other developments in the same area that you find attractive? What can you learn about the relationship between asking prices and actual sale prices in the area? Can you learn anything about the deals the developer has already made? With this information in mind, you can do a much better job of planning and going forward with the negotiation process.

If you have a real estate broker representing or advising you, he should help you with this. Even though real estate brokers have an incentive to make deals happen for higher prices (their commission tends to be based on price), they have an even stronger incentive to make deals happen—because unless there is a sale, there is no commission. If you are not using a real estate broker, perhaps you can get good advice from the bank from which you will be getting your mortgage. A local bank that understands the local market can be a tremendous asset.

If the developer has deep pockets and little incentive to sell quickly, that could indicate that she is not likely to move away from the asking price plus the incentives already offered. If local housing prices are steady or falling, if the developer has undertaken an aggressive sales campaign (advertising, other promotions or incentives, and so on), that indicates that she needs to make deals. Understanding these factors should help you understand what you can do.

In the meantime, you have to assess your own situation: How much can you afford to pay (including down payment, closing costs, mortgage payments, and whatever you will have to spend for decorating, furnishing, and moving)? Once you have this information in mind, you will know how much flexibility you have in terms of price. If the developer will take care of any decorating or customizing you need, that may be a good bargaining point for both the developer and you to use to reach agreement on price and other issues.

When a seller's offer is accompanied by incentives, or if incentives are offered without anything requested in trade, that means the overall package is just an opening gambit. Don't let the opening deter you from pursuing your interests; if the seller wants to make a deal, whatever you offer (unless it is totally unreasonable) is likely to bring about a counter-offer and a negotiation process that yields a mutually agreeable deal.

---

# He Agreed and Then Walked Away From the Deal

### From: Marcelo, Sao Paulo, Brazil

**Question:** *This week I made a mistake while I was negotiating. I had to bargain over a price with a teacher in a private class. I got 50 percent off the standard fee. He did not seem to be uncomfortable with the situation, so I thought that everything was okay. I had a commitment to have class with him the day after, but he did not show up. I called him, and he told me that another guy had asked him for the same time but offered a better price. He told me: "It is the law of supply and demand."*

*How can I know when I reach a price that makes both parties comfortable, so that I'm not betrayed like this again?*

**Response:** A successful negotiation is a process that leads to an agreement that each party will willingly fulfill. If your price negotiation with the teacher was imbalanced—if you pursued the agreement with enthusiasm whereas he moved toward agreement reluctantly—the negotiation was destined to fail.

Someone has said that a perfect compromise is achieved when all the parties leave the bargaining table equally happy—or equally grumpy. It may well be that during your negotiation with the teacher, you were not paying sufficient attention to his communication—not only his words, but also his gestures and body language. His mouth may have said yes, but his body may have been saying no.

Finding a way to reach an agreement about price very often requires bringing more factors than price alone into the negotiation. When you tell a professional who is paid for his time that the price they want to charge is too much in your eyes, while you may not be intending to do so, you are attacking his ego. For example, if a teacher says, "My time is worth 50 dollars per hour," and you say (in effect), "It is only worth 25 dollars to me," that can be viewed as an attack on his or her self worth.

Before you negotiate, consider all the interests of the parties and other stakeholders. Sometimes money seems to be the only issue, but more often than not, money's value is based on how it will serve a given party's interests—for example, ego, the capacity to pay existing bills, or an opportunity to buy something special. It appears you work for a bank. Are you in a position to offer the teacher advice on how to obtain the best services, a favorable loan, or some other benefit in which your expertise would be helpful?

As you go through the negotiation process, it is critical to keep asking questions. Ask other parties questions that will help you understand their feelings about the issues. Ask yourself whether you are doing a good job of meeting your own interests, and whether you would be happy if you were on the other side of the bargaining table. Unless each party to a negotiation feels the process is fair, there will be no real commitment.

Once you reach an agreement, it is important to have some kind of documentation so that each party knows his/her obligations to the other parties as well as the rewards he or she can gain from fulfilling the deal. You may not need a formal contract, but if you have an appointment with the teacher, you can ask him to write down the date, time, and payment due so that you have a reminder to put in your calendar. You may also want to respond with a simple note indicating your intention to be at the lesson on time, prepared to learn, and with payment at the appropriate time or in the appropriate form (check, cash, credit card, whatever).

Negotiation is not a competitive sport. Forcing a teacher to cut his price in half may feel like a "win," to you, but it may not motivate the teacher to keep the deal if he can get a better price from someone else. There should be incentives for each side to keep their part of the bargain. Otherwise, there's really no deal.

## What Do I Do When I'm Stuck With an Overpriced Car Mechanic?

### From: Pradeep, Chennai, India

**Question:** *Please suggest how I should negotiate with a car repair mechanic after I have agreed to pay him a set amount for the job, only to find out later that I could have had it done less expensively elsewhere? I accepted his quote on trust because I was referred to him and also because he was the nearest to the place where I had the accident.*

**Response:** It sounds as if you have found yourself in a very challenging situation; however, it is not hopeless. First, you should examine the circumstances and establish some facts:

1.  Have you used this car mechanic before?

2.  Can you communicate to the mechanic that you are looking for someone you can trust for the long term, to whom you can go for future repairs?

3.  Can you present a credible case demonstrating that you know many other car owners who would be interested in listening to your recommendations of automobile mechanics?

4.  Is there an association of car mechanics that has an interest in promoting and/or sustaining the good reputation of car mechanics as a profession? Can you find one or more mechanics willing to be your advisor in dealing with the mechanic who is working on your car? Perhaps they can help you with questions or other insights that might be significant in your discussions.

5.  Do you know of any private organizations or government agencies that exist to protect the consumer from unscrupulous business practices?

6.  You say that you went to this mechanic because you were referred to him. Have you discussed the situation with the person who referred you to him? Does this person have a long-term relationship with the mechanic? Can you ask this person to assist you in your efforts to improve the price?

7.  Is this mechanic attached to a dealership, or is he independent? Is he his own boss, or does he have to report to someone else?

If there is an existing or possible long-term relationship with the mechanic, he should be able to see that it is in his interest to treat you properly—to get your business in the future, to protect his reputation, and to keep himself on good terms with whomever recommended him.

With all these issues as background preparation, you should describe the needed repairs to several other mechanics and ask them for the price they would charge. If possible, you should get those price estimates in writing. If all the other estimates are far more favorable, you should see whether it is possible to cancel your agreement with the existing mechanic and have it repaired by someone else. I imagine this would be extremely unlikely, but you should still investigate the possibility.

Is the repair work covered by automobile insurance? Can you go to your insurance company and ask for their assistance? If you do not have insurance, it might make sense to find someone involved in car insurance who can give you a written estimate of the fair price range for the kind of repairs being performed.

Ultimately, you need to communicate with the mechanic. Approaching him in anger is not likely to yield a favorable outcome. Rather, you should approach him looking for information: How serious is the damage? Does he have experience with this sort of problem? What are the factors that were considered when the price was determined? Why is his estimate *different* (notice I do not suggest you ask why it is higher) from those of other mechanics in the region/neighborhood?

In my own experience, when my car needs bodywork, I take it to a more expensive mechanic. He offers guarantees and performs such extras as cleaning the inside and outside of the car when it is finished. Is it possible that you can give your mechanic an opportunity to prove that he is of better quality than his cheaper competition? Perhaps he can offer you a guarantee; perhaps he can wash and wax the car after it has been repaired; or perhaps he would like to have you write a letter he can post on the wall of his garage saying he did a terrific job, was very courteous, and so on. In other words, how can you make him want to have you become someone who will act as a reference in the future?

It is extremely difficult to change a contract once it has been executed. Both parties have to want to make that change. What does the mechanic have to gain by changing the price? If he has nothing to gain—neither reputation, nor long-term relationship, nor favorable publicity, nor credibility with the person who referred you—then it is not likely he will want to change the price. Asking questions is more likely to yield a favorable result than confrontation; perhaps you will hear him say something that triggers a creative way for you to convince him to change his mind.

If you can't get him to change the price, and you can't "rescue" your car and get it to another mechanic, you should look upon this as a most unpleasant lesson. Getting the mechanic angry with you could mean the repair job is not done as well as it should be. There is no magic formula to change a situation once it has been agreed upon. You did what sounded right at the time. Unfortunately, it may end up costing you more money than it should.

---

## The House That Might Own My Family

### From: Donna, Armonk, New York

**Question:** *We have been looking for a contemporary home in a town that has only been building colonials for the past few years. Normally, a builder builds a home and then advertises it. People rarely purchase land and hire architects and builders in this area because it is extremely costly. It has been suggested to us that the way to go about getting a newly constructed contemporary is to find a builder who has already purchased land, and then ask if he would build a contemporary or customize plans on a colonial instead.*

*We visited a model home that was built by the most well-known builder in the area. He also has the best reputation for quality. The layout was very nice and could easily be converted to a contemporary. It was just about the only home we've been interested in during our years of searching. Unfortunately, it was not in a neighborhood that we wanted to live in, so we asked if he could build it elsewhere, modifying the plans to a more contemporary look. He said he would only do it if he could also build other homes on the site. After calling him several times over the course of several months, he told us of some property that he had in a nicer area. He plans to build five homes there, but they wouldn't be completed for another year.*

*Because the lot is larger than the one on which the model was built, he said that he would have to enlarge this house and basically refused to build it the size of the model. He discussed changes that he could make, talking of opening up a wall to make a loft, adding contemporary windows and railings, and so on. We asked him the price, but he said he would have to call us. He would not even give us a ballpark. When he finally called us, we were shocked to find that his price was $145,000 more than the model. Granted, this is a more upscale neighborhood, and both the lot and house are bigger. He also said that this was the base price and anything else done to it (like those contemporary windows) would be an extra charge.*

*The house sounds beautiful and I think he knows how hard we've been searching for what we like. (We've actually been searching for years, and this is the closest thing we've found to what we want.) The seller's market here is excellent, as anyone can tell you. Houses cannot go up fast enough.*

*Because of the incredible demand, builders are building on the oddest lots—on steep hills, over streams, and so on. At the end of this particular property, there is a small stream running through it. It wouldn't be on the lot, but this still concerns us. We mentioned it to the builder and he didn't seem to think it was a problem. I wonder if he is fixing it and raised my home price to cover the costs.*

*We tried twice to get him to go down on the price. My husband was actually planning on spending $75,000 less on this house. (We were also hoping to adopt a child, and I don't see how that's possible if we pay this price.) The builder absolutely will not budge at all. Everyone I speak to says that it'll never happen because builders (especially this one) will always find someone else who will pay.*

*If we give in, there's no telling how much higher this price will go once we start adding extras. Also, I'm nervous about making a deal with someone who is not flexible, as we will have to be in contact with him throughout the home-building process.*

*I've checked other homes in the area and his price is most definitely the highest. Home prices have been rising at an incredible rate, and I think he's projecting into next year's prices—but who knows what they will be next year? The market could change at any time and interest rates could soar. How can I be expected to make a commitment when it's a year away?*

*Because we sought him out and we are the first people interested in this site, we even asked him if it was possible to lower our price somewhat and make up for it on the other four houses that he is building in this area. He told us that because we were picking out the best lot, he wouldn't be able to do this. We really want this house, but I can't see it happening if he doesn't lower his price. It feels very unfair, and whenever I think I might give in, I start to feel like a sucker.*

*I'd appreciate any advice you could give me. I would like to respond to him as soon as possible because he has recently cleared the land and put his sign up. I don't want to lose my chosen lot, so I'll have to work fast.*

**Response:** Frankly it sounds as if you have placed yourself in a spot that leaves you with extremely limited flexibility. The builder knows you are lusting after the land he has to offer; and you have let him know that your alternatives are virtually nonexistent. To be gentle, this is not a very good situation to find yourself in when you are negotiating.

The good news is that if you go forward with this particular builder, the site, and the house he can deliver, you have a clear idea of what you are going to get and a good guesstimate of how much it will cost. The bad or at least complicating news is that the financial commitment required by the house threatens your capacity to adopt a child.

You have to ask yourself several questions. What are your priorities? Have you any financial flexibility? Can you change your criteria for the house and/or location to bring things to a more reasonable price? Can you limit your financial exposure by deciding ahead of time what kinds of extras to include in the construction plans, and then stay away during the construction work so you don't make any expensive change orders during the process?

The picture you present displays tremendous vulnerability on your part; the best course you can take will be to focus on minimizing your costs while making sure that the commitment(s) you make do not make you a prisoner of the house, financially or otherwise.

---

## Is My Garage Mechanic Ripping Me Off?

### From: Adam, Ames, Iowa

**Question:** *I asked a mechanic to give me an estimate on my car's brakes, and even told him it was the driver's side brake that was giving me the problem. He looked at all my brakes, told me what was wrong, and then charged me $36 for the estimate. This charge would be taken off if I got my brakes fixed by him. I wasn't satisfied with the price he wanted to charge to repair the problem, so I didn't want him to fix it.*

*He never told me there would be a charge for the estimate, and nowhere did I see a sign indicating anything to that effect. I paid the $36 but I think this was an injustice. What, if anything, can I do about this? Can he legally do this without first telling me about the charge? I made it clear from the outset that I just wanted an estimate.*

**Response:** I cannot answer your question about whether the mechanic has the legal right to charge you for his estimate. The law of your state or community may govern that. The same is true regarding your question about the legality of charging for an estimate without a sign indicating estimates are not free.

However, you did ask him to spend time to examine your car and determine what repairs were needed. He most likely gets paid by the hour for his labor, so it is possible that the $36 represents the price of the time he invested in examining your car and preparing the estimate. Yes, he should have told you about the charge before undertaking the estimate. Whether what he did was fair depends on normal practice in your community; in many communities it is normal to pay for estimates, whether or not the work gets done there. You might ask other mechanics what they do. Another good idea is to check with other people you know who are familiar with local practices.

This is a situation in which using objective criteria can help you learn whether the situation you experienced is fair or not. Asking disinterested outside experts can inform you of normal practice in your community. If what the mechanic did is out of the ordinary, then it could make sense to let him know you are disgruntled and ask him whether he would be interested in doing business with you in the future.

In this case, normal local practice is the best guide to whether you were treated fairly or simply ripped off.

---

## Upgrading My SUV

### From: Cesar, Los Angeles, California

**Question:** *I just bought an SUV with leather seats and CD player, but that's all it came with. How could I go about asking the dealer for additional stuff for my vehicle, such as fog lights, at no extra money, if possible, or at a low cost?*

**Response:** If the additional stuff you want on your new car is something that occurred to you after the purchase was made, then your desire to add new features will require that you undertake a new negotiation process with the dealer. If you had asked for a car with those features before agreeing to the purchase, and the dealer said the CD player (for example) was not available, going forward with the purchase meant you were agreeing to accept the car as it was presented to you.

You should undertake two different paths of inquiry. The first is to explore alternative ways to acquire the accessories you want on your car.

It may be that what dealers call aftermarket features can be found at the dealership, as well as at stores that sell automobile parts and enhancements. Your second line of inquiry should be to try to figure out what your dealer might have to gain by agreeing to sell and install the new features you want at no or low cost. What benefits can this bring the dealer? Are you a long-established customer who has bought more than one car there? Can you promise to make a substantial number of future purchases? Can you deliver other customers? If you put yourself in the dealer's shoes, what would motivate you to do this favor for Cesar?

It may be that buying the additional accessories after buying the car doesn't cost any more than it would to have had them included in the initial package. If you can help the dealer find a convincing motivation for offering you a special deal, you may have a chance of getting what you want. Unless the dealer has something to gain, it is hard to think why s/he would give you a better price than any other customer.

## Take It or Leave It

### From: Liew, Singapore

**Question:** *What should we do when a customer says, "Here's my offer—take it or leave it"?*

**Response:** What you describe is a classic *positional approach* to negotiation. Your customer is locking herself in; she cannot change her mind without risking losing face.

First, it is crucial for you to have done your homework so that you have a sense of the range of prices that makes sense for you or your company. Second, you have to ask your customer *why*. However, if you simply ask why, at best you are likely to receive an answer that simply justifies the price she has named. So you need to ask indirect or more subtle questions to learn what interests lie behind the customer's approach. Some examples:

1. Can they do business with your competitors, with price as the fundamental determinant?

2. Does the customer have some personal issues at stake? Her ego? Orders from the boss? The need to meet a quarterly quota?

3. Are there other issues beyond price that deserve attention, such as quality, delivery time, an ongoing or new business relationship, the extent to which your product will fulfill the customer's needs?

4. What is your BATNA, your Best Alternative to a Negotiated Agreement? Do you need this customer for reasons similar to the issues raised in points 2 and 3?

5. What would happen if you asked your customer, "From what you are saying, am I to understand you do not consider it is in your interest to make a deal with me?"

In order to prepare for a customer from whom you expect this sort of response—or for any negotiation, for that matter—you should look to your interests; to those of your customer or customer's representative; and to the interests of both of your constituencies, the other possible stakeholders in the deal. This sort of preparation will help you develop a negotiation strategy focused on the questions you need to ask to derive the information you need in order to make the kinds of proposals or responses most likely to satisfy the most important interests of the stakeholders.

## Selling Projects in a Down Economy

### From: Raja, Kuantan, Malaysia

**Question:** *I work for a construction management company specializing in development and contracting works. Currently we are negotiating and trying to develop a proposal with federal and state government agencies to put up various facilities. We know they are in dire need of these facilities, but they are undecided because of the cost factor. The economy in Malaysia is not good at present. We need your invaluable advice on how to conduct a winning negotiation with client. We need that magic word to convince the client in this "down" economy.*

**Response:** Your question is in many ways the fundamental question most salespeople must face: How to convince someone they need what you have to offer. There's both good news and bad news here. The bad news is that there is no such thing as a "magic" word that is guaranteed to produce results. The good news is there are things you can do to try to move them from your "prospect" file into your "client" file.

You've made it clear in your question that the projects your company would like to undertake are all quite needed. While there may have been indications of the importance of the projects at various times in the past, have circumstances changed? Were the priorities spelled out when there was plenty of governmental funding? Is the support from the projects coming from above or below? You also need to take a look at the interests of the various parties. For example:

- You are interested in bringing income to your company and, consequently, to yourself.

- Your company's owners want income to assure the company's survival. They may also be interested in the prestige of being able to point to a particular project and say "I built that."

- Employees want to be paid for their work.

- People in the general public have an interest in having good facilities to use; they are also likely to be concerned with how much they pay in taxes.

- Government officials might be concerned with political ramifications, budgetary constraints, credibility with their constituents, relationships with contractors, and so on.

There are probably many constituencies to add to this list. In addition, all of the interests listed above are assumptions on my part. When you map out the interests of the various parties, you must make assumptions, but you must be careful not to be governed by your assumptions. You need to do a reality check on each of your beliefs to learn whether it really is an interest of another party and, if so, how important it is to them.

You learn about interests by asking questions and then listening. The more attentively you listen to the people you want to convince, the more likely you are to respond with language and ideas they will find appealing. If you listen well, you will probably learn things that you might never have considered that you can "sell" them on.

Given that the economic situation is a problem, your success could well depend on figuring out the priorities in the minds of government agency decision-makers. Which projects are most important? Which areas need to have government impetus for employment? What long-term financing possibilities exist? Are there projects that might be supported by international agencies, by private-sector users who need a better facility to aid their businesses? What allies can you find to help encourage favorable decisions by the government people?

You face daunting challenges; I do not envy your situation. But I have a feeling that doing a good job with your homework can increase the likelihood of your success, and in that I wish you good luck. As the American inventor Thomas Edison once said, genius is 99 percent perspiration and one percent inspiration.

# Chapter 7

# Negotiating Across a Divide: Culture, Gender, and Other Factors

---

## Understanding Cross-Cultural Negotiation

### From: Quynh, Adelaide, Australia

**Question:** *I'm currently working on an assignment on the need for managers to understand cultural diversity, and cross-cultural negotiation is one of the points I'm going to talk about. I was wondering if you had any information on the topic, please.*

**Response:** If there's one fundamental point to make about cultural diversity and cross-cultural negotiation, it is that *it is increasingly risky to make assumptions about other people based on labels*. Further, someone may not "look" Australian, even though his or her family has been in the country for several generations.

In negotiating with people from different backgrounds, the most effective approach for overcoming possible communication barriers is to focus on the interests of the parties. Why do they want what they want? You have to go behind the justifications they may use to defend why they want something; after all, virtually everyone can come up with a justification for whatever they want. The real issue is *how* what they want will serve their interests.

Managers need to understand the people they work with. Without clear mutual understanding, it is almost impossible for a team to reach its objectives. Even in a relatively homogeneous organization, designers and accountants, for example, may be seen as representing different cultural perspectives. Getting them to work effectively together is obviously crucial for a company's success. Most assuredly, getting people whose cultural diversity is based on different issues is no less important.

One has to be careful not to pigeonhole people, to assume that everyone with a particular "label" thinks or acts alike. If it weren't for differences, the world would be a very boring place. What we need to do is find out how different interests can be addressed to yield results that work for the parties who have the ultimate responsibility to implement the agreement. Cultural diversity, whether based on profession or tribe, is simply one of the elements that need to be taken into account to keep things operating on a civilized level.

## Does Cross-Cultural Negotiation Have to Mean Conflict?

### From: Jaclyn, Melbourne, Australia

**Question:** *When it comes to cross-cultural negotiation, it seldom seems to be a collaborative mutual learning experience; rather, it seems to be considered solely as a means for resolving conflict. What is your opinion on that? I would love to find or understand some strong arguments on both sides of the problem.*

**Response:** Virtually every negotiation can be viewed as "cross-cultural," whether it is between parties from different national backgrounds, different departments within an organization, or even different generations within a family.

Calling a negotiation cross-cultural does not detract from the fundamental nature of the activity. Successful negotiation is a process by which parties reach an agreement that each is committed to fulfill. Different kinds of people have different styles of getting to agreement, whether the styles are derived from the market for raw materials, the different ways men and women communicate, or the reality that people in sales and people working as purchasing agents have very different ways of looking at issues.

If we regard negotiation as an activity that brings parties together in a process that helps bridge cultural gaps, it can be used to resolve conflicts, develop collaborative solutions to shared problems, or find common ground for taking whatever next steps make sense for the parties. Cross-cultural negotiation is a collaborative mechanism for learning about another party's needs as well as a civilized mechanism for resolving disagreements. Each of these analyses applies.

Don't worry about finding a single definition for cross-cultural negotiation. Instead, use the process to help yourself or your team make progress toward agreements that work.

---

# Dealing With a Tough Member of the Opposite Sex

### From: Cyril, London, England

**Question:** *In the course of my consulting work, I cover for my boss during his absence and have to deal with his peer in the customer organization. She is an unpleasant person, to say the least. When my boss is not present, she will not engage in any type of conversation—a "good morning" or "hi" or "how do you do" are always met with a minimal response and retreat. Perhaps she feels that if she deals with subordinates like me, her position could be undermined within her own team and my status raised in their eyes.*

*When my boss is away, I meet with her weekly to discuss our performance as consultants. This one-on-one meeting is always at her office, across a table. I have tried to maneuver my position so that we are sitting on the same side, but she will always pick a confrontational position.*

*During the meeting, if all is not well, she is quite good at pressure tactics and tells me what my responsibilities are as her representative of our consulting firm (in other words, everything that fails is my fault). On the other hand if our firm has not had sufficient notice of the requirements to be able to deliver, this is not her problem. In these situations she gets her team into the meeting, as she says, "to sort things out." Usually this ends up with about five people and her arguing about different versions of what did or did not happen. As the only representative of my firm, I get bullied. During a confrontation and in her presence, the people on her team change: They tend to lie and become very economical with the truth; certainly, they never challenge her judgment.*

*She is very clever at using her attributes as a woman to gain control—standing or leaning into my personal space, adjusting my tie or removing a spot from my jacket. At times, if she is not getting the results she requires, her bottom lip will droop and she will almost break into tears.*

*What can I do to even this situation out? My boss has the exact same experiences, by the way.*

**Response:** Based on what you've told me, here are some suggestions to help get you started:

1. You indicate your boss has the exact same problems. Maybe the two of you can consider some sort of strategy, both short- and long-term. For example, you might consider doing the good-cop/bad-cop routine.

2. One question is, who needs what from whom? Obviously in a service business, one must always keep the customer enthusiastic; however, is she throwing her weight around because she has real power, or is her company under contract for three more years and she is just playing out some personal power trip?

3. You mention that she uses her attributes as a female to do things that a man is much less likely to do with/to another man: adjusting your tie, removing a spot from your jacket, invading your personal space. It's similar to the situation in which the maitre d' has seated you with the sun glaring in your eyes: if you let him do it and don't let him know it makes you uncomfortable, then in effect you are asking for "it"—in this case, not only the tie-straightening behavior, but also whatever other more serious invasions she undertakes on your dignity. You have every right to say to her, "When you adjust my tie, I feel uncomfortable. Only my wife/mother/mother-in-law normally does that." Or—and this is the heavy weaponry—"How would

you feel if I adjusted your clothing without being asked to do so? Could that be viewed as sexual harassment?" Another possibility is, "You know I realize this is ridiculous, but a member of the staff might see you adjusting my tie and could draw an incorrect conclusion about the two of us. I thought you should know that it could give a false impression."

4. When she raises substantive issues—for example, that your failures to deliver the goods make your firm look bad—this is a chance to put active listening to work. Ask incisive questions: "What do you mean by that?" "What have you observed that could be changed to yield a better result?" "Why is this important?" and so on. And then listen carefully to her answers. Learning about her interests may help you figure out a way to present resolutions that are more appealing to her, at least on a demonstrable basis.

5. Do the people she works with rejoice that you (and your firm) are the whipping boy? Do they suffer the same kind of treatment when you are not around? They may not be able to deal with you directly on business issues, but I wonder whether there is any way to learn from them in more general conversation.

---

## Girls Will Be Women! Negotiation Hot Buttons

### From: Awni, Bethlehem, Palestinian Authority

**Question:** *How can semantics, emotions, attitudes, and gender bias affect negotiations?*

**Response:** Thank you for your terrific question. Negotiations are profoundly affected by the factors you raise. Everyone has hot buttons that can lead them to focus on emotional issues rather than the subject matter of a given negotiation.

More than 25 years ago, a relative of mine was negotiating to buy some property from a women's organization, the YWCA, for a commercial real-estate project. My relative and one of his business associates were the only men in the meeting; the YWCA's representatives were all women. It appeared the parties had basically reached agreement, when my relative said something like, "So it looks like you girls are ready to agree." All hell broke loose. The business associate started kicking my relative under the table; one of the YWCA people said, "There are no 'girls' here! We are women!" My relative turned to his business associate and asked, out loud, "Why are you kicking me?" Then he said to the YWCA representative, "I don't know why you are so sensitive; if you were men, I could have called you 'boys' and no one would have taken offense." The business deal fell apart as a result of my relative having activated the hot button of another party.

Negotiation is the process by which human beings exchange items of value in a civilized manner. In response to your question, *human beings* is the operative phrase. People make assumptions about themselves and about the people with whom they negotiate. Making an assumption is risky; when we assume, we take the chance of making an *ass* out of *"u"* and *me*. If we pigeonhole people, if we assume that everyone from a particular ethnic group, gender, profession, company, or whatever is going to respond in a predictable way, we are not treating them as individuals, but rather as objects. In negotiation we may well walk into the process with assumptions, but we have to test whether those assumptions are valid *in each and every case*. Some women may indeed be comfortable being called girls (although I haven't met any in the past few decades), but some may not. We need to ask questions and listen to the answers to find out whether our assumptions are valid.

It is also critical not to give offense in the negotiation process. When you are negotiating with someone new, it is important to say something like, "I don't know you very well, but I do know that as we negotiate, I have no desire to offend you. If I say or do something which troubles you in any way, please let me know. I would consider it a great favor." After you say that, you and your negotiation partner are sharing a mutual obligation to be open about peripheral issues that might otherwise detract from the central issues of the negotiation. You—or they—may still make mistakes. But hopefully the initial indication of good faith may mitigate those potential hot-button issues.

# What About People From Brazil?

### From: Brigitte, La Defense, France

**Question:** *I would like to know more about negotiation with people from Brazil. Generally speaking, do Brazilian people use an integrative or distributive approach? How is their culture different, and what kind of mistakes should we avoid with them in particular?*

**Response:** Your question is troublesome because it seems to be based on the assumption that upon finding out one is negotiating with someone from Brazil, it is immediately possible to predict all kinds of characteristics about him or her. Brazil is a very large country with a large and highly diverse population. To assume that there is a single "Brazilian style" of negotiation is unfair to the many individuals who call themselves Brazilians.

Rather than entering into negotiations with people or companies from any particular country assuming that "they all act alike," it is crucial to ask questions about the specific parties with whom you'll be negotiating. Find other people who have worked with them and ask for their experience and impressions.

More importantly, consider the wide variety of interests and styles that may drive your negotiation partners before you begin the process. Use those thoughts to develop a series of questions you can ask so that the people with whom you negotiate can let you know more about themselves (and thus help you understand what approaches are most likely to be convincing to them).

The best way to avoid making mistakes with any new person or group with whom you will be negotiating is to ask them to let you know what they find troublesome or offensive. While they may not tell you everything, what they say and what they don't say may be equally revealing.

It is extremely risky to generalize about people based on such external qualities as their nationality, their appearance, or even their gender. In our global community, an increasing proportion of the population is exposed to widely varied input from all kinds of sources. The global village is replacing the isolated hamlets where our ancestors once spent their entire lives.

# Tell Me About Americans

## From: Beatrice, Kuala Lumpur, Malaysia

**Question:** *Could you please advise me on negotiation with Americans? What approach do Americans use during negotiation? What kinds of mistakes should we avoid at all costs?*

**Response:** Americans are a very diverse group of people. Our population includes people from virtually every cultural group in the world. Thus, it is particularly risky to generalize about a specific "American style" of negotiating. That said, there are some general points to keep in mind:

1. People who are natives of the States or who have assimilated the general American culture tend to be annoyed by people who are dishonest. There is an American saying: "If you cheat me once, shame on you. If you cheat me twice, shame on me."

2. While many Americans can be very hard-nosed in their negotiation style, the concept of interest-based negotiation (often called win/win) is increasingly popular. This is a reflection of the belief that unless the parties to a negotiation are more or less equally satisfied with the result, the parties may not fulfill the deal with equal enthusiasm.

3. Like many other peoples, Americans do not like to lose face. We do not enjoy being embarrassed in front of other people, whether it's the parties with whom we are negotiating or others who are observing the process.

4. When an American asks a question, he or she usually wants a direct, honest answer.

Many other characteristics can describe how Americans negotiate. Each individual is a unique person, just as people are everywhere else in the world. So it is crucial to ask questions and then listen very carefully to the other party's answer to develop an understanding of why a particular objective is important to him or her.

## Comparing Asian Nations With Western Nations

### From: Massumi, Johor, Malaysia

**Question:** *I'm doing a research project on the different negotiating styles of Western nations and Asian nations. My job is to compare and contrast their respective styles. Would you give me some tips or any articles that I can refer to?*

**Response:** I find it hard to feel comfortable generalizing about Asians or Westerners as distinct groups. Even within my own family or group of friends, it seems dangerous to generalize about traits that are peculiar to men or to women, to the old or the young, to the Boomers or the Millennials.

Once when I was co-teaching a negotiation skills class in Singapore, my Indian co-teacher and I had an unrehearsed debate. He introduced the idea that Asians care more about relationships than do Westerners. I told him and the attendees that in many cases, that is the exact opposite of what I had witnessed. In both the West and the East, people are concerned about *ego*. In some cultures that is called saving face; others do not recognize or address the issue explicitly, but the same essential elements are there. Sometimes the cultural concern appears to be helping the other side save face, while in other cases, the focus is on saving one's own face.

The fundamental issue is that everyone carries a substantial amount of cultural baggage. By the same token, with the influence of global business and communications, cultural influences are increasingly shared and disseminated. It is quite risky to assume that because someone is from a particular background, he or she necessarily thinks or acts in only one way.

Given all this, in a negotiation it makes more sense to look to the interests of all parties involved, and move beyond presumed cultural barriers by focusing on the end results desired by the parties, and why those results are important to them. When you're dealing with people you don't know, it's crucial to make sure you are not treating them according to cultural stereotypes. By the same token, it is fundamentally important to find out whether they find certain things you say or do offensive, and to let them know what offends you in turn.

The world is divided into an incredible number of paired opposites: east and west, night and day, male and female—and this is not even the tip of the iceberg. Within what people refer to as the "West," one can find a myriad of cultural differences and nuances. Even if you take a single country, such as France or Germany, you will find differences of language, religion, and even corporate culture.

In short, generalizing about people is a risky endeavor. If we treat people as individuals, we are far more likely to find ways to convince them through negotiation.

## How Can a Man and Woman Negotiate With Each Other?

### From: Kurt, Salem, Oregon

**Question:** *I want to know if men and women differ in terms of how they negotiate. Are there differences in psychology, behavior, and communication? Are there certain things I should be doing when I negotiate with a woman that I should not do with a man? And conversely, what should I do when I negotiate with a man that I should not do with a woman?*

**Response:** Be careful not to assume that consistent sets of rules apply to all males or all females in terms of negotiating. Other differences between the parties may be more influential than gender; age, ethnicity, nationality, strong feelings about particular issues, and the subject matter of the negotiation are just a few of those issues.

To be on the safe side you might want to take a look at your assumptions about men and women, as well as any you might draw from literature. Then use those assumptions as guidelines when you start digging for information from the person with whom you are negotiating. Ask questions that will help you find out whether those assumptions are accurate. Find out what is really significant to the other party or parties, irrelevant of their gender or other differences. Your negotiation can then focus on interests, both yours and theirs, and you are far more likely to reach a mutually agreeable conclusion.

# What About Italians?

## From: Selena, Charlotte, North Carolina

**Question:** *I have an Italian client. I am about to negotiate a project and need some help on negotiating with Italians. Would you give me some advice, please?*

**Response:** It is tempting to make generalizations about the negotiation styles of people from different countries. However, just thinking about Italy, several questions come to mind: Is the party a man or a woman? From which section of Italy? What sort of educational background? What is his/her political situation in his/her company? How comfortable is she/he negotiating in English? As you can see, there is a virtually infinite number of questions you could ask, because everyone is an individual. What may hold true for one woman from an urban area of North Carolina may not apply to another woman from the same area or even of the same general demographic.

The important thing is to come up with a wide variety of questions that are designed to yield information about your client's interests and concerns. Asking open-ended questions and listening hard and seriously to the answers will reveal far more about his or her negotiation style (and the likely possibilities for resolution) than any pigeon-hole assumptions one might have about Italians in general. Perhaps the most important question to ask your client is "How would you describe your negotiating style? Are there elements of communication or interaction you find particularly convincing, offensive, or confusing?" You should encourage your client to ask you about your own negotiating style, too. Of course this requires figuring out what your style is before the question is raised.

Asking questions shows you are interested in other people. Listening well makes that point even clearer. No matter what a person's cultural background, having others pay attention to them is a gratifying experience that can lead to more civilized negotiation.

---

## Are There Statistics Indicating How Often People From Different Countries Disagree?

### From: Margarita, Bremen, Germany

**Question:** *I am an MBA student currently researching the average costs that companies incur when negotiations fail due to misunderstanding between two different cultures—for example, when an American company negotiates with a French firm. Do you know of any statistical data on the number of companies that fail to close their negotiations because of other cross-cultural differences?*

**Response:** I have no idea if there are any statistics relating to the issues you raised. Frankly I doubt there are any statistics about "failed" negotiations within companies, where there is a single culture, much less between parties from different countries.

Part of the problem is that developing such statistics presents virtually insurmountable problems. For example, in your personal life, how many times have your negotiations with family members failed to reach a mutually agreeable result? Can you blame those "failures" on differences such as age, gender, or education, or the simple fact that while you wanted to eat at an Italian restaurant, your brother or sister preferred Chinese? How can you prove that any particular factor was the most influential on the outcome?

In short, there tend to be too many variables at play in any negotiation to tease out the causative factor(s) for "failure."

---

## What About Different Business Cultures?

### From: Surendra, London, U.K.

**Question:** *What is the role of business culture in international negotiation? How important is it?*

**Response:** Business culture is a central element in negotiation. Every company has its own corporate culture. Thus, some companies are focused on short-term results while others look at the long term. Similarly, companies vary in terms of their treatment of employees from different backgrounds, dress codes, criteria for performance reviews, and so on. Within a given company there are often discrete "silos" or "tribes" that have a hard time reaching agreement with one another.

Businesses can reflect the surrounding or prevailing culture of the nation(s) in which they are based but you cannot take this as a given. The impact of national cultures on business varies enormously, particularly now that more and more companies operate in the global marketplace, with employees drawn from an ever-widening variety of national, ethnic, religious, and demographic backgrounds.

In negotiation it is crucial to avoid getting trapped by prejudiced expectations of how a person from a certain background (whether corporate, national, or ethnic) will behave. Focusing instead on the interests of the stakeholders will help you overcome cultural barriers, both real and perceived, and derive agreements that lead to mutually favorable outcomes.

---

## How Should One Negotiate With Vietnamese People?

### From: Helen, Passaic, New Jersey

**Question:** *I need some advice on negotiation with the Vietnamese. What kind of mistakes should we avoid?*

**Response:** When you negotiate with people whose culture is very different from your own, do your homework: Talk with people who have experience negotiating with people from that culture. Find books that focus on cultural taboos or customs. And be careful not to assume that everyone from Vietnam—or any other different cultural milieu—is totally predictable. Many Vietnamese people have been educated in the West, and are familiar with foreign corporate cultures. People raised in major cities may be different from those with a more rural background. Men and women may be sensitive to different issues. In other words, it is risky and possibly even insulting to assume "they all think alike."

The most important thing is to keep an open mind, ask questions, and invite the other party to let you know if you do or say something they find offensive. And you should do the same with them, being open about your "hot buttons."

---

# Can the Internet Teach Me How to Negotiate?

### From: J.J., Seoul, Korea

**Question:** *How can I, as a non-English speaker, practice my negotiation skills on the Internet?*

**Response:** Practicing negotiation skills via the Internet is most likely to be rewarding if the negotiation is real, rather than an exercise. Negotiation is a low-tech activity; we can use high-tech means of communication (e-mail, fax, Instant Messaging), but we will only do a good job if we have developed the kind of skills that work well in face-to-face situations.

The danger of using high-tech tools to learn negotiation skills is that so-called interactive electronic media are limited by their nature. Those mechanisms cannot reflect the wide variety of choices one can make regarding strategy, tactics, and techniques in a real-life negotiation. Negotiation is not like an airline pilot's pre-flight checklist, in which only one answer is correct for each element of the process. The dynamics of negotiation change all the time, even with the same person. People who are married find that their spouses are not always predictable; the same is true in business and other negotiations.

I do not have any fast or easy answers regarding learning negotiation in languages other than English. My first book, *Negotiating Skills for Managers* was published in a Korean edition. Perhaps that will help you.

# How Can I Deal With Chinese Tactics?

## From: Meg, Melbourne, Australia

**Question:** *I need some advice on how to counter Chinese negotiation tactics and strategies. For example, the Chinese often use the 36 stratagems and The Art Of War (Sun Tsu). For example, the idea of "killing with a borrowed knife." How do you counterattack or defend yourself against this strategy?*

**Response:** The most important element of your response to such strategies is to anticipate and understand them. In your example of "killing with a borrowed knife," you are talking about one party co-opting another party's strategy, tactics, or strengths in a pre-emptive manner in order to turn their advantage into your own. If you understand the tactical approaches another party is likely to use, or actually uses, in a negotiation, you will not be surprised, and you can think of substantive responses to their strategy.

You can also take a very different approach, not as an alternative but rather as a complement to the idea of needing to understand their tactics. You need to develop your own negotiation strategy based on a philosophy or set of ethical standards with which you are most comfortable. In ancient times people waged war to determine who was right—the winner, if you will—but now, most civilized people recognize that war is fundamentally destructive to everyone involved.

A negotiation that yields a winner and a loser is a failed negotiation. The "loser" is going to walk away grumbling, *If they think I'm going to fulfill my part of the deal, they're going to have to drag me kicking and screaming through the process.* There's an old expression in the United States: "If you cheat me once, shame on you. If you cheat me twice, shame on me." Negotiating is not an alternative form of warfare; rather, it is a full-blown substitute for the combative approach for solving problems.

If other parties insist on negotiating using outmoded competitive negotiation strategies, make it clear that you are not interested in a one-sided outcome. Unless the parties to a negotiation reach a mutually agreed-upon solution to which each is genuinely committed, the process was unsuccessful. You can say to the folks relying on *The Art of War*, "If you persist in using that approach, I am afraid we may fail to reach agreement." Because failure means a loss of an opportunity, they may realize that competition is not the appropriate direction to take. Negotiation by formula only works when the circumstances fit the particular formula. For negotiation to succeed, people need to accept that unless both sides are comfortable with both the process and the results, bullying tactics may win the battle but will lose the war.

## What About Malaysians and Venezuelans?

### From: Charlotte, Sydney, Australia

**Question:** *I need some advice in terms of negotiating with Malaysians and Venezuelans. What kinds of buyer-seller relations do they employ? Should I expect extreme behavior from either of them? What elements of their cultures are essential to know about before I begin negotiations?*

**Response:** I don't have a magic answer regarding the negotiating habits of people from different countries. The global marketplace, student exchange experiences, and many other factors mean that you can't always tell what to expect from a person based on their passport. One text you may find instructive is called *When Cultures Collide*, by Richard D. Lewis. It is the best one I have found.

Using interest-based negotiation is an excellent means for overcoming cultural barriers. It focuses on the fundamental reasons people pursue particular objectives, rather than getting lost in style.

## Getting Russian, Japanese, and American Negotiators on the Same Page

### From: Elena, Rostov, Russia

**Question:** *My company plans to negotiate with Japanese and U.S. partners. I would be grateful if you would advise me on the skills required for a successful outcome.*

**Response:** It is easy to fall into the trap of concluding that *all* Americans, *all* Japanese, or *all* Russians negotiate according to a fixed set of national or cultural norms. There is no question that negotiation styles among the three nationalities do vary—but then, there are also differences between men and women from the same country, between the old and young, and so on.

You need to inoculate yourself and your negotiating teammates against stereotyping, and be open to the possibility that the other group's negotiation styles will be different from your own. Americans have the reputation for wanting to get to the bottom line right away; Japanese negotiators are often characterized as being unwilling to say no because they don't want to make another party lose face. In addition, many Americans are receptive to touch (handshakes, pats on the back), which is generally quite different from Japanese behavioral norms. Your cultural inoculation should be based on a simple concept: "Don't get hung up on style."

Do your best to understand your interests and your BATNA (Best Alternative to a Negotiated Agreement). Ask yourself why you want a particular result, and whether there is only one way to get there. Prepare for the negotiation process by doing the best you can to figure out what the interests and BATNAs of the other parties are likely to be. Then use the process to do a reality check on whether those assumptions are accurate. Think about why you are negotiating with the other teams. Compare negotiation with weaving: if you weave many strands together, you produce a more durable fabric (agreement) than if all the ideas come from a single direction.

During the negotiations, keep reminding yourself why you are there. Focus on your own interests: "How will this answer or proposal serve my interests?" That way, you can avoid being confused by issues of cultural dissonance. For example, the Japanese party keeps saying yes, you should ask, "Does this mean you are ready to sign an agreement with me right now?" Explain to them that if they say yes but mean no, it could cause you to lose face with the other negotiating parties or within your own team. If the American negotiators try to rush you into agreement, rather than getting angry, it would make more sense to say, "My/our decision-making process has to work in the following way [and then explain it as clearly as you can]." Keeping the negotiation process transparent, making sure all parties understand what is going on, can reduce the likelihood that cultural differences will cause things to fall apart.

Keep asking yourself questions: *Why am I here? Why did he ask that question? Is my answer going to serve my interests or hurt them? Did he/*

*she say that to annoy me, because it is a common negotiation tactic in their country, or because they really intended to make a point with which I happen to disagree?*

Negotiation success depends on bringing together the ideas and contributions of people who are coming from different angles. Recognize that people differ for all kinds of reasons—and that those differences can contribute to a better agreement.

---

## How Can We Avoid Causing Offense in a Multinational Company?

### From: Daniel, Hong Kong

**Question:** *Our company has branches all over the world, among many different cultures and nationalities. How can I call members of our staff into one meeting/negotiation without risking doing something disrespectful to the various cultural traditions at play?*

**Response:** My very simple answer is based on taking your question literally. An invitation to a meeting should not represent too many opportunities for cultural dissonance. If the meeting is taking place in Hong Kong, with attendees having to travel great distances, clearly you have to ask questions to make sure that travel arrangements, meeting times, and even menu items for meals are offered in a way that gives participants choices that respond to cultural differences. Thus, for example, making sure there is an alternative to pork on a lunch or dinner menu is crucial.

If your question is really more about how to avoid making cultural gaffes during a meeting, it makes sense to check with headquarters staff for hints based on their experience with different cultural groups. In addition, it is respectful to ask meeting attendees in advance if there is anything they might find offensive in terms of timing, agenda items, dress code, or other cultural factors. If you indicate your concern *before* the meeting, you are demonstrating your openness and sensitivity to the possibility that different people from different backgrounds have a variety of concerns. You are demonstrating your good faith and your intention not to cause problems based on cultural issues.

Remember that nationality is not the only potential cultural divide. People from different "tribes" within an organization may have varied cultural sensitivities, too. Sales, purchasing, design, manufacturing, human resources, and other professional groups tend to have particular ways of looking at things that are different from those from other departments.

Ask many questions during the meeting planning process. Continue to ask questions that look for sensitivities as the meeting goes forward. After the meeting, get feedback from participants so you can learn for the future.

One of the most effective ways to bring corporate culture together and rise above the "natural" cultural divides is to undertake collaborative learning programs in core competencies. My experience in working with multinationals has been extremely positive. Training people from multiple national and professional cultures creates a common bond among them that builds an effective and shared corporate culture.

---

## Is Cross-Cultural Noise the Real Problem?

### From: Sally, Melbourne, Australia

**Question:** *I'm trying to understand the following statement: "The key task of cross-cultural communication is to limit the noise in cross-cultural interaction."*

**Response:** Limiting cross-cultural "noise" shouldn't be viewed as the key task. What you want to do is reduce cross-cultural *dissonance*. Fundamentally negotiation works best when the parties use the process as a means of exchanging information. If cross-cultural dissonance hampers information exchange, negotiation is more difficult.

Crossing cultures may reflect personal communication styles that derive from one's nationality, gender, age, or even membership in a particular corporate tribe such as sales, accounting, or manufacturing. Because "tribal" characteristics can come into play in any negotiation, a good negotiator needs to go beyond what she finds on the surface to develop a better comprehension of the interests of the other party or parties.

A successful negotiation is a process that leads to an agreement the parties will willingly fulfill. Unless the confusion that can arise from cultural dissonance is overcome, each party's difficulty in understanding the other could create obstacles to agreement, because external factors have created a smokescreen that gets in the way of understanding.

## We Have Conflicting Rules for Doing Business

### From: Summer, Tianjin, China

**Question:** *How should I respond to orders from a U.K. customer who doesn't follow our normal business procedures? He wants to open a letter of credit before sending samples to us, which is not something we will typically do.*

**Response:** If I understand your question correctly, you and your British client have opposing expectations of how business should be done. The real question is how to resolve a situation that arises when business customs differ.

When two parties disagree on the best way to move forward in a business transaction (or any issue requiring agreement, really), it is best to take a step back from the problem and focus on the process of resolution in the context of your interests. You and your British customer have different expectations of the best way to do business, but if you take a look at the situation and focus on the interests of each party, there is an excellent chance you will find that those interests can complement each other. Once each party realizes that, it can increase their motivation to devise a process that works for each.

In this case, you and your customer both have an interest in doing business together. The question you have to ask one another is not "Which one of us is right and which one is wrong?" but rather "What can be gained by solving the letter of credit/product sample issue?" In fact, each party needs to go deeper to understand why a particular outcome is important to the other. Does your customer need the protection of a letter of credit because of financial or legal concerns? Does your company need samples in order to investigate what resources you will need to fulfill the ultimate business agreement? Both you and your customer need to exercise empathy; try to understand why the other wants the process to go according to his/her rules. Discuss the possible reasons underlying your customer's position with colleagues within your company, with other people you know who have done business with the customer, and, if possible, with British nationals who might be available to give you their insights on how business transactions should go forward.

After doing this research, your next step should be to ask your customer questions that will yield information about what is driving his decisions. Remember to ask open-ended questions; questions that can be answered with a yes or no won't yield very much useful information. Asking questions can be a sign of respect; it shows you are interested in the other person and take him/her seriously. Given the cross-cultural aspects of your situation, you should be particularly interested in finding out whether your customer is troubled by any of your business customs. If something you do bothers him, that doesn't necessarily mean it is wrong, but perhaps you could modify your approach or style of communication so that the procedural obstacles can be reduced.

Crossing cultures, whether within a single company or across the globe, virtually always means that people think differently and interpret things in different ways. If you demonstrate to your customer that you have an open mind and can act with some degree of flexibility, perhaps it will build his confidence that he, too, can bend a bit to satisfy interests that are important to you.

Globalization can bring tremendous benefits to many people. However, it also increases the opportunities for confusion and difficult communication. Pursue information, increase your flexibility, and look for trade-offs between you and your customer. Tell him, "If you do something specific that I find favorable, then I will reciprocate and do something that will respond to your needs."

## The Importance of Apologies

### From: Rosaria, Melbourne, Australia

**Question:** *Could you help us resolve a question facing our employees who work in a restaurant? One of the workers is an Aboriginal and he wants all his coworkers to sign a "sorry book" to commemorate the so-called stolen generation—the Aboriginal Australians who were stolen from their home*

*areas and subjected to forced assimilation into the European culture of the
majority of Australians. How should I deal with this situation?*

**Response:** Before addressing the specific question you raise, it is very important to understand that apologies are phenomenally important in negotiation. In all human communication, there's a risk that one or more of the people involved might say or do something that the others will find offensive. Sometimes there is a history of bad relations between specific people, between companies, or, as in the case you describe here, between different cultural or ethnic groups. When an apology is appropriate and genuine, it may not wipe out perceptions of past wrongs, but it can establish a sense of good faith between people who might otherwise have had a difficult time with each other.

People from certain cultural, ethnic, or national groups may have a chip on their shoulder about what they perceive as past wrongs. How significant this chip is needs to be questioned before you make a decision on how to deal with it. In the case of your restaurant, you need to ask whether there is a potential impact in signing the "sorry book" that extends beyond your restaurant. For example, what have other businesses in Melbourne— or across Australia—done when presented with the request for the apology for past wrongs to Aboriginal people?

If you and your colleagues sign the book, what impact will it have on your business? What effect might it have on relationships within the restaurant staff? Are there any members of the staff who feel there is nothing they need to apologize for? Did the person who wants the book signed present the idea as a suggestion, a request, or a demand? While it is unlikely that any members of the restaurant team actually participated in the government-sponsored harm done to Aboriginal people, it may well be that you and most or all of your colleagues feel that those actions were, indeed, bad behavior. If that is the case, and if signing the book will make your Aboriginal colleague happy, it's hard to see how signing the book could create a problem.

On the other hand, if there are differences of opinion, you need to figure out whether the relationship with your Aboriginal colleague is important enough to override disagreements and be a strong enough motivating factor for the team to sign the book. In other words, you need to look at what interests are most important to you, and figure out whether the relationship is more important than any concerns about how the idea of the "sorry book" was presented (friendly or hostile).

Apologizing by signing the "sorry book" may indicate that the signer's ego is not troubled by the gesture of apology, and it may help heal painful personal or communal memories that truly bother your colleague. Open discussion can make the process work better. Apology only hurts the ego of someone who is insecure about his or her self-image.

---

# Why Are Many Women Hesitant Negotiators?

### From: Debbie, Quincy, Massachusetts

**Question:** *Many women (not all) refrain from negotiations in the work place. Why is this, and how can they overcome this fear or hesitancy?*

**Response:** There are many theories and books that examine the real or perceived differences between men and women. In the workplace, historically women have been treated as second-class citizens for so long that many women have been socialized to accept low expectations for themselves. Luckily this is changing. In many professional schools, such as law and medicine, women outnumber men, and a growing proportion of the current female portion of the workforce feels far more empowered than previous generations.

Nonetheless, in a workplace where men still tend to dominate, the odds are that women (or any other group of people not fully represented at the decision-making level) will feel less able to influence members of the dominant group. This can even hold true in cross-silo decision-making in corporations: If a company is sales-driven or focused on cost-cutting, people from other elements of the business may feel less able to influence decisions. The question of why women may feel hesitant about standing up for themselves can have a multiplicity of answers. The real question is, what can be done about it?

Someone who is well-prepared for negotiation will feel far more confident and will actually be more competent than someone who flies by the seat of his/her pants. Of course, preparation takes work, but it pays off big time.

Anyone going into a negotiation, whether male or female, should make a list of all of the potential stakeholders in a given decision, and then write that list on a flipchart, whiteboard, or even a sheet of paper. Thereafter, it is important to try to figure out what each stakeholder's interests are likely to be, as well as how to address those interests during the negotiation process.

Preparing is not a solo activity; colleagues may well have good ideas or insights to contribute or helpful criticism to improve the preparation. You'll have to accept the idea that not all of the assumptions you make will be accurate. A more knowledgeable colleague might be able to steer you away from an inaccurate assumption or at least help you do a reality check without locking you into a perspective that can kill your strategy if the initial assumption proves inaccurate.

Use this preparation process, which I call the Negotiator's Interest Map, to help you figure out what information you need from your negotiation counterpart in order to be able to present him/her with a solution that responds to both your interests and his. Remember that negotiation is not a competitive sport. You certainly want to have your interests served, but you won't get very far if your counterpart walks away from the negotiation feeling grumpy, unfairly treated, and unwilling to fulfill the bargain. This sort of preparation can build your self-confidence and help overcome the reluctance that so many women—and people in general—feel about pursuing their interests in negotiation.

Asking good questions and encouraging others to talk, not only yields information but also shows an interest in them as human beings—and even a degree of respect. There's an old saying: "Talk to a man about himself and he can listen for hours."

Going into negotiation well-prepared can make an enormous difference in one's self-esteem and capacity to go forward.

# Chapter 8

# Legal Issues, Disputes, and Deadlocks

---

## It's My Fault, but I Can't Pay

### From: Wantty, San Juan, Puerto Rico

**Question:** *Two weeks ago I got into a car accident. I was coming out of the driveway and hit another car. He was speeding down a street (at about 50 miles per hour) that has speed limit of 25 miles per hour. Since he was going very fast, his car pushed my car to the right, which hit another parked car. The police said it was my fault because the other guy has the right of way. My insurance won't pay anything for the accident because I sent in my payments late. Thus, the other party is asking me for $4,000 to repair his door. "Parked car guy" wants $3,000 for his backlight and bumper. I've asked them to get other estimates and they said they did and they both want original parts for their cars.*

*Right now, I think I can only come up with $600 cash total. I am a second year optometry graduate student who has no savings or assets under my name. I have a lawyer friend who told me that if they do take me to court, they would have to hire a lawyer, as that's the law in Puerto Rico. I seriously do not have any money to pay them and am thinking about going to court.*

*Any suggestions and advice?*

**Response:** It sounds as if you're between a rock and a hard place. I am surprised that your insurance company is off the hook because the accident was your fault. While insurance laws vary from jurisdiction to jurisdiction, a basic purpose of car insurance is to protect a car owner from the financial consequences of problems he or she causes. The other surprise to me is that the victims' insurance coverage does not cover underinsured motorists. Since you don't have any assets to cover their damages, in some states, at least, their insurance should provide coverage. So you have some homework to do with the local government agency that governs automobile insurance to find out whether these issues are really as you describe them.

In the worst case, if neither you nor your victims has any coverage, and you have no assets with which to compensate them for the damage (which, under the law, you caused), it would make sense to think about some sort of long-term compensation. Although $7,000 is far more money than you can produce at the moment, once you are working, perhaps you can provide regular monthly or quarterly payments that will ultimately compensate the other car owners for the damages they have suffered. If you demonstrate a good faith intention to do your part, perhaps they will find some way to reduce their expectations.

Your bargaining position is strong in that you have nothing, and the cost of litigation for your victims could be prohibitive. However, perhaps one of them has a relative who is a lawyer, so that may not stop them from pursuing you in court. The more serious question is one of ethics. If your action did indeed cause harm to others, there is a moral issue involved. Shortcuts like bankruptcy may work but do nothing for your personal reputation, much less your own self-image.

I hope the insurance companies have an obligation to give their policyholders value for the money they have spent on car insurance premiums.

# Now That Her Husband Is Dead, They Want Her to Pay More

### From: Jeff, Flower Mound, Texas

**Question:** *My sister's husband recently passed away at age 47. They had two car loans through their credit union at very good rates. Now the credit union wants to close those loans and have her establish new loans in her own name. The new loans would be at considerably higher rates. The higher payments will be an enormous financial burden on her, added to the emotional burden she already feels.*

*She is willing to continue to pay off the loans with the same monthly payments they made when her husband was alive, but the credit union insists that it is their policy to terminate the loan. It doesn't seem right to me. My sister and her husband have been loyal customers for years but that doesn't seem to make a difference. What should she do?*

**Response:** You need to find out what the state and federal laws say about the right of a lending institution to terminate loans due to the death of a spouse. It is also appropriate to ask the credit union to send you a copy of the loan agreement, pinpointing where it indicates that your sister and her husband agreed that the death of either would trigger a loan termination.

It would also make sense to analyze the BATNAs (Best Alternative to a Negotiated Agreement) available to both your sister and the credit union. For example, how would the credit union feel if this situation were published in the local newspaper, circulated to local clergy, or otherwise given publicity? You and your sister should start some quick and serious research on alternative loan sources, both locally and in the broader market. In other words, if your sister and the credit union cannot reach agreement, what are her alternatives?

You may also want to find out whether the loss of her husband has had any impact on your sister's credit rating from credit rating agencies. For example, if her financial situation has not changed significantly, one has to question the financial justification for the credit union's proposed action—other than greed. If her income and/or assets have suffered, then perhaps the credit union is justified as viewing her as more of a credit risk.

Look at the impact of the credit union's proposed action on all the stakeholders: your sister and her family, other members of the credit union, the credit union's competitors, and whoever else you can think of who will be affected by this decision. For example, what would your senator and representative in the state legislature think about this, and what action might they take?

The odds are that the legal situation is stacked against your sister, and others in similar situations. However, it is worth finding out whether these penalties are applied to men who lose their wives. If men and women are treated differently, that could give your sister an interesting variety of potential choices.

---

## The Mining Company Wants to Shaft Me

### From: George, Nova Scotia, Canada

**Question:** *I worked for a mining company underground for 25 years less 41 days. The company announced closure and gave out 25-year pensions. Because I worked 41 days less than 25 years, I received no pension at that point. After they laid everyone off, they decided to keep the company going but with a reduced work force. I injured myself on December 5, and since then I have been on worker's compensation. According to the doctors, I'm going to be on it past my 25-year point. Is there anything I can do? (Incidentally, this company was owned by the federal government of Canada, and was a Crown corporation.)*

*Because I did not take my severance as of yet, the company has been calling me to come in and take it. I told them that I wasn't ready yet, but they said that I had to go in and sign off by Jan 28. In the sign-off form, you state that the company is not responsible for anything and they cannot be held liable for anything. Now in Nova Scotia, people on worker's compensation cannot be terminated from their employment, or so I am told. My question is, should I sign the company's form or should I wait until I'm off worker's compensation?*

**Response:** You're facing a challenging situation. Perhaps some of these thoughts can help you take appropriate action.

If you belong to a labor union, I'd imagine you'd be in touch with whatever department the union has relating to worker's compensation, retirement, and the other issues you've raised. If you are *not* a union member, it could make sense to go for advice to a number of possible sources: the provincial employment service; local lawyers with expertise in labor relations, workers compensation, and retirement; people you've worked with who have some experience with these issues; or perhaps your favorite member of the clergy.

Because you are in Canada, I can't advise you on your legal rights and obligations. But, because the company wants you to sign a legal document, you do need to know what those rights and obligations are before you can make an informed decision. In the United States, most lawyers do not charge anything for an initial visit. You might want to visit a number of lawyers to see which one(s) seem most compatible with you. Again, your friends and neighbors may be able to tell you which lawyers are most likely to be helpful.

On the face of it, I cannot understand what you would gain from signing the company's document. Are there any benefits they can withhold from you if you don't sign? If their deadline is simply a "Do it by then or else," you need to ask yourself, friends, and coworkers—and the company— "Or else *what?*"

Keep your personal interests in mind, and don't let the apparent power imbalance force you into any unwise decisions or actions.

---

## We're Splitting Up, but I Don't Want to Leave Our Business

### From: Kathy, Waterloo, Illinois

**Question:** *My soon-to-be ex-fiancé and I entered into a bar business three years ago. We are buying the place bond for deed after leasing for a year. All licenses and bills and the corporate name are in his name only. We have the bond for deed in both our names. Things are not working out and he wants to sell, but I have worked too hard to give this up. What can I legally do?*

**Response:** I haven't a clue what "bond for deed" means, but the fundamental facts you present are fairly clear. If I understand you correctly, you want to end the personal relationship and, despite your fiancé's desire to get out of the business, you want to continue with it.

What follows is not legal advice: It would make sense for you to attempt to negotiate with your fiancé to reach a settlement each of you is comfortable with. One approach could be to offer to buy him out, thus obtaining ownership of the corporate name, the licenses, and other corporate assets and liabilities. If the bar has not been profitable, your fiancé may well be pleased to get rid of its indebtedness or other liabilities.

You need to think about your BATNA, your Best Alternative to a Negotiated Agreement. Would it make financial sense to a) buy out your fiancé for a payment right now, b) pay him off over time, c) buy the corporation out of bankruptcy, or d) take over the corporation with its liabilities and let him off debt-free? Would you be better off letting the existing business disappear and, once it is closed, starting over again in the same location? I recognize the licensing issue could be a challenge in this situation, but you must have a reasonably clear idea of the choices and challenges you face.

Do the relationship issues stem from the business, or has the business relationship deteriorated because of your personal issues? Would you and your fiancé give the same or similar answers to those questions?

You need to separate business and personal issues, prioritize your interests in each case, and then focus on how the choices you can make will serve or harm those interests.

---

## My Wife Wants to Divorce Me—From My Inheritance

### From: Matt, Long Island, New York

**Question:** *My wife and I are going through a divorce. We have been married for five years. She has a master's degree and makes $51,000; I make approximately $35,000 per year. I do however, have an inheritance which she sees as a big target. This money is supposedly untouchable because it is not marital assets; yet she and her attorney are focused on it just the same. She wants my* *inheritance money, but I honestly feel that there are no legitimate marital assets to split. She wants $75,000, and I want to give her zero. What is the best way for us (with our attorneys) to break this deadlock? Is this a case of flinching? She has nothing to lose and everything to gain no matter what.*

**Response:** The law of your State has a decisive influence on what assets can be considered in a divorce settlement. If your inheritance has always been treated as a separate asset to which only you have had access and which has only been used for your benefit (for example, you have not used inherited assets for a down payment on a house for you and your wife), the ownership of the asset should be easy to define.

To me the question is, what is the basis of your wife's claim on your assets? Will you be responsible for alimony and/or child support? Has your wife, with the larger earned income, contributed more than you to the day-to-day expenses of your household? Has your wife saved any money from her earned income that she would have spent if you were not contributing to the household accounts?

This may indeed be a case of flinching, or a game of "chicken." From an objective standpoint, can you imagine any justification for your wife's claim to a share of your inheritance? Is $75,000 a significant portion of the inheritance, or does it simply equal the annual income taxes paid on the inheritance? This is a question of perspective. How much is it worth to you to get closure on the relationship? If you have no children, what is it worth to you to get on with your life with no overhanging burdens?

If your lawyer and other (perhaps more objective) observers feel you have no legal or moral obligation to part with any of the inheritance, are there any justifications that might convince you to the contrary? If the worst thing that can happen is that your wife and her lawyer threaten to drag out the process, will your additional legal fees and other costs approach $75,000? Remember that unless she has free legal services, extending the length of the process costs her just as it costs you.

The money may have to do with a question of fairness in both directions. If that is the case, you should choose to take the fairest route. If it is simply a question of either spouse using the money to express vindictiveness, then fairness is not the issue, and sheer cost/benefit calculations should guide your decision-making. Remember, as F. Scott Fitzgerald wrote, "Living well is the best revenge."

---

# I'm in The Middle of My Parents' Divorce

## From: Chris, Anaheim, California

**Question:** *I have been given 50-percent ownership of our family's engine machine shop. My folks are getting a divorce and I want to purchase the remainder of the business from them. Pop, who still works in the business, will accept payments from me over time; however, Mom wants her share now so that she can move on and eventually open her own business.*

*Here is where it gets complicated: the divorce settlement will consist of Pop giving up all interest in their jointly-owned house and me coming up with a lump sum to pay for Mom's share of the business. How do I get her to take less for her share in order to make this more affordable for me?*

*I do feel I have a few good cards to play. First, if she wants to force a sale of the business, Pop and I will walk, and I don't think anyone would buy knowing that 25 percent of the workforce is leaving. Second, she is walking away with more money at one time than I will ever see out of this business; she leaves, and I get the bill. I don't deny paying for the remaining percentage, but let's not be greedy for it all at once.*

*How can I get her to take less while realizing that she is getting a good deal?*

**Response:** The most important thing to do is to ask your mother for a face-to-face conversation about how best to deal with the situation. There are an awful lot of questions you could ask that just might help you devise a proposal that works for both of you.

Before raising the questions, I am curious: when you were given the 50-percent share of the business, who was the owner who made the gift? If it was your father alone, was this something he did to keep you in the business? Was it done in contemplation of the divorce, as an attempt to reduce the assets vulnerable to a divorce settlement? Also, who owns the other 50 percent? If it is your father, there may be a possible deal there—but that may mean he still has to pay your mom from his proceeds of the sale. If it is your mother, that can have one set of ramifications; if it is someone outside your family, that's another matter.

So here are some questions to address:

- What is the market value of the business? You may find that a business broker or some other disinterested third party can do a fair appraisal that will mean that neither you nor your mother is pitting one person's opinion against the other. The market value of the business should be appraised both in its present condition (with you and your father continuing to be involved) and in its possible future condition (after you and your father quit). The money such an appraisal would cost should be well worth the investment. If both you and your mother pay 50/50 for the appraisal, neither of you can say: "It was your appraiser, not mine, who concluded that was the value of the business." What if your father were to join in paying for the appraisal?

- When your 50 percent ownership was given to you, was there a value placed on the gift by any taxing authorities? Did any parties have to pay any taxes on the gift?

- Has a court made any determination of value? Has a court determined a deadline for concluding the financial elements of the divorce?

- You should ask as diplomatically as possible what your Mom's feelings are about your future. What kind of relationship does she want to have with you? What interest does she have in your capacity to survive and, hopefully, thrive financially?

- Does your mother need a particular amount of money to get her new start in life? If you cannot supply the entire amount she wants from you in the form of a purchase price for the business, would you be comfortable cosigning a bank loan using all or part of your share of the business as collateral?

- While she may want lots of money immediately, how would she feel if you offered to pay a little larger total, but spread the payments over time?

- Sometimes parents use their children as pawns to punish each other. Is this relevant to your situation?

To sum things up, Chris, you need to listen hard to what your mother indicates about her interests—why she is pursuing her various objectives. What you learn from her may be tremendously informative, opening doors to ways to devise creative ways to solve the problem you are facing.

## He Wants My Money but It May Not Be Mine

### From: Jeanine, Trumbull, Connecticut

**Question:** *I am divorcing my husband, and every time he gets upset he says he is going to take all or half of the money my father left me when he passed away. It is all in my name, but my brother and sister need to receive a portion of it. It is all tied up in T-bonds. My mother and father were separated for more than 30 years but are legally still married. I was, however, the executor of my father's estate. Can I claim that because my mother and father were still married, the money is really still hers?*

**Response:** You need to figure out whether your husband's insistence on taking the money is a negotiating ploy or a legitimate possibility. The whole issue may be out of his hands—or yours—depending on the laws governing such funds in your state.

One question in my mind is, if you have control over the money, but your brother and sister need a portion of it, why have you never given them their share of the funds? If the law says you cannot touch the money during the divorce process, it may be too late. On the other hand, if you can distribute funds to your brother and sister, even though your own share might be at risk, unless by some weirdness they are parties to the divorce, it seems unfair not to distribute their funds to them. Then, while the remainder may be at risk in the divorce, at least your brother and sister get their fair share.

If you have a lawyer, you should rely on her/his advice on the legal issues. Without legal representation, you run the risk of bargaining away assets that are not properly yours. Don't do this on your own.

## Our Representatives Made a Bad Deal and Victimized Their Fellow Union Members

### From: Catherine, Hayward, Wisconsin

**Question:** *During contract negotiations my union's representatives did not bring back to the union the full information about the offers the school board* *was presenting for the contract. They only brought back the offer that benefited them and took money from the majority of the union. What action, if any, can I take against the reps who negotiated unethically and benefited monetarily from doing so?*

**Response:** There are several approaches you can take; each requires that you (and those who agree to work with you) do some homework and ask some questions. The first set of questions relates to the union and its rules:

- Are there any union bylaws that outline the responsibility of union representatives to report on all offers made by the school board?

- Are representatives required to provide progress reports before reaching agreement with the board?

- Are they obligated to provide an explanation of the various offers and counter offers that occurred during the negotiation process prior to a union vote to accept or reject the contract?

- How does the rank and file feel about the situation you describe? Would they agree with your conclusion?

The next set of issues you need to investigate relate to the nature and accuracy of the information you have:

- Are you, or is anyone you know, in possession of documentary evidence of the more attractive offers made by the school board during the negotiation process?

- Do you have evidence that anyone (union representative or school board member) misrepresented information in a fraudulent manner? This is a heavy-duty issue, as it could have criminal implications.

Next, you have to think about the long-term consequences:

- Are any of the "bad guys" up for reelection or reappointment anytime soon?

- What would happen to them if their constituents came to believe that the union representatives behaved unethically?

- Would the school board members be thought of as heroes for having saved the taxpayers money? And, would that "heroic" status be threatened if union members made noises indicating a likelihood they plan to a) vote against the agreement, or b) raise a ruckus in some other way?

In many ways, doing a proper job of negotiation reflects what is known in law as *agency*. Negotiators are often effectively agents for their constituents—or, to use the legal term, their *principals*. In the case of a school union, that may be a bad pun, but the fundamental principle remains that an agent's obligation to his/her principals is absolute; the agent cannot act for his/her own benefit if it runs counter to the interests or objectives of his/her principal. If an agent cannot accept the principal's objectives or interests, then the agent should resign from the agent/principal relationship. In negotiation, one must consider the three classes of stakeholders: negotiators, constituents, and other interested parties (OIPs). If there is a conflict of interest between a negotiator and one or more of his/her constituents, that conflict must be addressed before the process of formal negotiation goes forward.

Not knowing the details of the story you present, I am not comfortable drawing any absolute conclusions. You should consider who the stakeholders are, what their interests are likely to be in the situation, and whether any moral or ethical obligation has been breached. The questions raised previously may give you hints of direction you might take, but you must be careful to ascertain whether the allegations are true and whether the agent/principal relationship has been handled improperly.

---

# He Makes Promises, Then Waffles on Delivery

### From: Dave, Las Vegas, Nevada

**Question:** *I got a grade in a class in school that was below a B. I negotiated with the teacher to allow me to resubmit two assignments. The teacher told me I did well on the resubmits and I would get at least a B grade for the course. My problem is that the teacher hasn't changed the grade. I am getting nervous. He seems to be waffling on changing the grade. I don't know what to do. Can you provide some advice?*

**Response:** First you should learn as much as you can about the process a teacher has to follow in order to change an existing grade. He may face some significant bureaucratic rules about changing grades. If this is the case, you may want to approach him as a potential partner, offering to do whatever paperwork you can to assist him through the process.

If the grade-changing process is not that complex, you should learn about the rules your teacher has to follow in terms of satisfying his immediate supervisor(s). You should also try to discover as much as you can regarding his grade-changing history: Has he had to do this before? Does he have a negative reputation within his department or school relating to changing grades? In other words, is there any chance that changing your grade might be troublesome for the teacher's professional reputation? If that's the case, you may want to meet with him and discuss the issues he faces and brainstorm together ways to overcome the problems.

There is also the chance the teacher is lazy; once the term is over, he wants to get away on vacation and not bother with paperwork. Here it might be a good idea to let him know that you are prepared to be persistent until he fulfills his promise to you. That may motivate him to get you off his back on this issue. You may also want to ask him what he faces in terms of the grade-changing process, thereby discovering his interests and objectives as they relate to your situation. Ask him what he is trying to teach you by making promises and then waffling on fulfilling them. Needless to say, do this very diplomatically!

As a last resort, you should investigate what kind of appeal process is available through the school's administration. You need to determine whether you can succeed at getting the grade changed through that process—and whether it will advance or have a negative impact on your interests.

# Farmers' Roadblocks Tie Up
# Roads in Poland

### From: Pawel, Warsaw, Poland

**Question:** *At present we are having a lot of strikes in Poland. Could you give me recommendations on how to prevent such events before they cripple a country?*

**Response:** I've just returned from a business trip to Europe, where I read every day about how farmers have erected roadblocks and stopped traffic on major highways in Poland. To use the American expression, it is very difficult to put the toothpaste back into the tube once it has been squeezed out.

Clearly it is important for people in any country to listen to each other and explore possible issues that can form building blocks for agreement. In a young market economy, people often focus on only what is in their own short-term personal interest, which can make cooperation difficult. Of course, this is often a problem in mature market economies, as well.

If I were the king of Poland, I would get relevant leaders from government agencies and farmers' organizations to spend time learning about the process of negotiation, focusing on mechanisms for learning how to work together to respond to the interests of the parties at the table, as well as those of their constituents. Polish farmers are crucial players in the economy and the international credibility of your country. To a great degree, they also are what enable the Polish people to survive by having enough good food to eat. Governments have to deal with those issues as well as many others. As the two sides learn how to understand everyone's interests, they may find there are potential building blocks for agreement.

In the short term, each side needs to find confidence-building measures. So one side may ask, "If I do [x], then will you do [y]?" It can help to take one step at a time to build the habits of reaching agreement with each other.

These possible approaches have not solved the immediate problem. But I would suggest that as people develop an understanding of the long-term interrelationship of the interests of relevant parties, they'll be more likely to reach agreements that are both wise and efficient.

---

## Breaking Deadlocks in Labor Negotiations

### From: Lee (Labor Union Representative), Singapore

**Question:** *We are negotiating a collective employment agreement. For some benefits, the management has refused to move from their stand. These are not unreasonable benefits. They are present in most of our unionized companies. We are willing to compromise and change the components of the benefits, but management still refuses to budge. We are not willing to give up either. At one point, the manager said her points and I said mine and then we remained silent. Is this a good thing?*

*In Singapore, if there is a deadlock, we can refer to the Ministry of Labour for third-party intervention. But how can I go about cooling down the whole situation and making management see my point? I have to say that the woman who was negotiating was really rude and attempted to undermine my power.*

**Response:** Here is what has happened in a nutshell: in spite of your willingness to modify your demands, in response to a similar modification in the conditions offered by the management representative, the situation has unfolded as follows:

The two sides stated their positions, after which there is silence. Silence is often the most appropriate response to an unacceptable proposition. What complicates matters further is that in your eyes, the management representative has behaved rudely toward you and has also effectively undercut your power and perhaps even your credibility with your constituency.

In negotiation, "position" is a dirty word. Someone who takes a position is effectively saying, "Do it my way or it won't get done." One possibility in your current situation, in which you and the management representative have withdrawn to neutral corners before resuming the attack, is to say to her, "We have each done a good job of describing our positions, the result each of us wants as an ideal consequence of our negotiation. Now it is time to take a step back and look at why each side feels it's position is the best answer. In other words, why does the deal between us have to contain the elements each of us has described to each other?"

What you are looking for are the interests underlying the positions you've taken. When you find interests, it is often possible to discover some common ground. Both labor and management want to keep the business operating because it yields profit for the owners and wages for the workers. There may be other shared interests, as well: a belief in the product or service that is produced, matters of pride in being affiliated with the company, a desire of each negotiator to prove to his or her constituency or boss that he/she is competent, the desire of the negotiators to save face, and so on.

Take these common factors and see whether they can be applied to elements of the negotiation, to begin to build them into elements of an agreement. "If we agree on this point, let's shake hands on it and implement it and see whether that gives our bosses/constituents a measure of confidence in us." Or perhaps this is a situation in which the negotiators have to build confidence in each other. Confidence-building measures can give each negotiating party an initial set of "wins" that gives him/her the confidence that there is something to gain in continuing to work together toward a resolution.

One complicating factor, which you don't describe specifically may be that the negotiators have parted in an unfriendly manner. And perhaps each is unwilling or fearful of re-opening the process. You have to ask yourself whether you have a BATNA, a Best Alternative to a Negotiated Agreement, with this party. If you do, then it may make sense to head in that direction. If you do not, if you *must* reach an agreement with this party, then you have to find a way to reopen discussions without saying, "Okay, I accept your view of things, now you can beat up on me some more."

You must let the other party know that you are a human being with dignity and honor and that you have a strong enough sense of self-worth to be able to say, "Okay, our previous negotiations have not gotten us to a mutually satisfactory agreement. Let us meet to discuss the negotiation process, the ground rules for behavior, and, after that, set up a different time to negotiate the tangible issues following those behavioral rules."

I often recommend that people read a good negotiation textbook to get a quick fix on some basic negotiation strategies. While reading a book is nowhere near as helpful as getting trained in negotiation, it is better than nothing. After you read the book, you may want to make a gift of a copy of the book to the person with whom you must negotiate. "This book describes the style of negotiation I tend to use. Because I hope we can understand each other better, and because I am not trying to pull a fast one on you, here's a copy of the book with my compliments to help you understand me better." Giving the gift may well be a face-saving way of saying, "Let's get back together and see if we can be co-creators in solving the issues in front of us."

One secret in all this is to leave your weapons outside the negotiating space. Separate the people from the problem. After all, even if you could "erase" the person with whom you are negotiating, the issues would still remain.

---

## Communicating With Fragmentary Bargaining Units in Labor Negotiations

### From: Bill, Dallas, Texas

**Question:** *Several years ago the airline I work for was struck by the union representing its flight attendants. Since that strike, management and union leaders have attended various programs to improve relations. One program, offered at Northwestern University, was centered on conflict resolution. Management and the union leaders "adopted" interest-based negotiation techniques as they prepared for upcoming contract negotiations. Since the strike, joint management/union committees were formed to deal with attendance problems and scheduling improvements. These committees appeared ineffective from the start.*

*Does interest-based negotiation work well when you are dealing with union employees who are scattered across the nation, who are basically unsupervised, and who do not interact with managers or others "in the know" on a daily basis? That is, can employees who are not well-informed of the industry in which they work or goals of management be expected to make rational, interest-based decisions in contract ratification votes?*

*It is my opinion that interest-based negotiations are effective when dealing with work groups that interact with management on a daily basis. Employees are better informed as to the company's goals and understand the business of the company better when management is interacting with them.*

*With my airline, you have an unsupervised work group that is basically iso-*
*lated from management by the nature of the work environment. The distrust*
*that flight attendants (and pilots) have toward management is amazing. The*
*union, its leaders chosen from this group, tends to distrust management,*
*too. Any proposal made by management is greeted with skepticism, and this*
*skepticism is communicated to the membership.*

*Management knows its employees are disgruntled and, as the airline has*
*already stated in a trade magazine, it does not know how to deal with it. I do*
*not see interest-based negotiations being effective with a membership that is*
*unattached to the core of the business.*

**Response:** Thanks for your most thoughtful and important question. You
are right. People who espouse interest-based negotiation are thinking, for
the most part, about situations in which the most interested stakeholders
are at the table. However that is not the whole answer. One must approach
bargaining considering the interests of stakeholders who are not at the table
as well as those in attendance.

At first glance, interest-based negotiation seems problematic in resolving the issues at your airline. Before you turn your nose up at the approach,
however, I suggest you consider whether the "wham, bam, thank you,
ma'am" approach to bargaining is any better than or, in fact, nearly as good
as the interest-based approach. The real issue is how best to implement interest-based negotiation when it is impossible to get everyone to the table
at the same time. This may require asking some creative questions, such as:

1. Can cabin crew members discuss issues during quiet times on
   flights, layovers, coffee breaks, and so on?

2. Is there a mechanism in place for survey research by management, the union leadership, or as a joint undertaking by the
   management and union representatives directly involved in the
   bargaining?

3. Is it feasible for the rank and file to circulate opinions and
   suggestions that ultimately bubble up to the top? Think of
   the Committees of Correspondence during the American
   Revolution. Perhaps the union or management should set up
   a Website offering stakeholders a chance to consider and comment on proposals. Perhaps you and your colleagues could set

up your own Website(s) and invite other employees to brain-storm together.

It may be worth asking whose interests are being served by keeping the communication process as it is now. If individuals are avoiding being representatives of their constituents, should those individuals be replaced through democratic elections or other legitimate mechanisms? Americans live in a representative democracy. Except for some small towns in New England, the town meeting is a thing of the past. And even in many New England towns, representatives are elected to the post of Town Meeting Member. Winston Churchill called democracy the worst system of government in the world, except for all the others.

If the chief executive is on record as feeling troubled by how to handle employee communications vis a vis labor contracts, you might send him a note with specific ideas of how to improve the situation. Interest-based negotiation works best when people exercise creativity; it sounds as if this is a case where that is true in spades.

In a more general sense, negotiation is easier when smaller groups are involved. Former senator George Mitchell's changes in the number of people involved in the Northern Ireland peace process is an excellent example of this approach. However, we can't always attain the ideal. In the case of flight crews that operate independently of each other, it may be that both management and the union have an obligation to work together to reach out to the membership and foster the kind of communication that can lead to a constructive and mutually rewarding agreement.

# Chapter 9

# The Worst of the Worst: Sticky Situations, Problem People, and Nasty Negotiators

---

## She Won't Talk to Me

### From: Jane, Las Vegas, Nevada

**Question:** *I just started a new job and have only been there one week. All of my coworkers seem nice, but one of the women is a dental hygienist who refuses to speak to me, even when I address her directly. How can I resolve this problem?*

**Response:** If the dental hygienist treats everyone else more courteously than she treats you, you need to ask your coworkers whether there is sort of a breaking-in period before she starts communicating with newcomers. Find out whether she is shy or whether she needs to play some sort of ego trip to protect her self-image. If she has a habit of treating newcomers with silence at first, ask your colleagues for advice based on their own experiences. You should also ask whether any of them observed anything in your behavior when you first arrived that might have led to the current situation. For example, perhaps the hygienist doesn't take kindly to folks who call her by her first name without having asked permission.

Take a close look at yourself and try to figure out whether there is anything unique about you that might trigger the silent treatment you are receiving from her. Does she harbor any known prejudices that might lead to the silent treatment you are receiving? Examine your short- and long-term interests in the relationship. Do you have anything to gain from communicating with her? Do you need information from her, approval from her, or data that she controls? If you have no particular need to deal with her, perhaps you should be polite, but remain clear in your own mind that, essentially, she does not exist in your world.

After looking at all of these factors, perhaps it would be worth finding an opportunity to be alone with her and ask her straight out what's going on. Admittedly that can be difficult. To build up to that you should find out whatever you can about things you and she might have in common: taste in music, sports, food, leisure time activities, or even professional issues. That way you'd have something to talk about so that your initiative to break down the stone wall is not just for the joy of hearing her voice.

Finally, think of your interests: why you are concerned? Try to figure out what has driven her decision-making. And, above all, *listen*.

---

## Her Low Self-Esteem Holds Her Back

### From: Bruce, Chicago, Illinois

**Question:** *I'd like to better understand how to deal with someone I know who perceives herself as the victim. This is a person who believes that someone is always doing something to hold her back, which is why she can never get ahead. What she doesn't realize is that she is one who is causing the issue that is preventing her from moving forward.*

*This to me appears to be an issue of poor self-esteem. Still, it gets very frustrating working with someone like this. We're always trying to help her feel better about herself, so that she will see herself in a better light, but it doesn't seem to work. She's a long-term employee so she's not going anywhere; she'd likely have the same issues in any other job she held.*

*Any suggestions on how to effectively deal with this person?*

**Response:** Your first obligation is to yourself and your company. Let's call the troublesome woman "Rapunzel." You need to examine the impact

Rapunzel has on office productivity and relations among other employees (with each other), as well as the extent to which her self-perceived victimhood interferes with a good workplace atmosphere. Does Rapunzel's personality problem interfere with her own job performance? If the answer to that is yes, is there a consequent negative impact on others' work?

While this may sound a bit harsh, if you conclude that Rapunzel's attitude is simply an annoyance, perhaps you can also conclude that trying to change her is not a high priority. Under those circumstances, you and your colleagues might make a game of the situation by including Rapunzel's personality traits as part of her make-believe job description and looking for opportunities to pat yourselves on the back and say (under your breath, of course), "There she goes again."

Of course Rapunzel's low self-esteem is no joking matter. More than likely she is a very unhappy person. Unfortunately, unless there is an in-house psychiatrist who can work with her, you and your colleagues could be making a serious mistake in attempting to treat her problems. Since it sounds as if Rapunzel needs qualified professional help, unless your workplace is equipped to offer that kind of help, you will be expending resources with little promise of a favorable outcome.

If her attitude is doing demonstrable harm to productivity and morale, you ought to examine how Rapunzel can be taken out of the loop when her self-image exacerbates problems. At the same time, the humane thing to do is to figure out how her problems can be treated by a professional. Perhaps, to help her save face, finding an approach that doesn't single her out yet leads her to the kind of help she needs would accomplish your objective of helping her get better.

It sounds as if your office has adopted a very caring approach to Rapunzel. It also sounds as if it has not been working. You and your colleagues are not to blame if she does indeed have a personality disorder. When you negotiate it is critical to pay full attention to your own interests, because unless you take care of yourself, you can't do a good job of caring for others. Your interest in Rapunzel's well-being is certainly kind, but if it detracts from your own sanity, that does not serve your interest or that of your company. And taking on the role of psychiatrist might even be having the exact opposite effect from what you intend.

I don't envy you or your colleagues—or Rapunzel—in this situation. But it is crucial to be realistic about everyone's interests, not just those of Rapunzel.

---

## Her Petulance Is Disruptive

### From: Christy, New Kensington, Pennsylvania

**Question:** *We have a woman in our office who is older, but she acts as though she were still in high school. If something doesn't go her way or she is told that she is incorrect, she doles out the silent treatment until she feels that you are "ready" to be talked to again. It causes a lot of tension in the office because it is a constant, ongoing thing with one person or another. You can't tell her that it is immature, because she is always right and no one else ever is. What do you do in this situation? Ignore her altogether, sit back and let her do this to everyone, or just ride it out? Please help!*

**Response:** The old expression "you can't teach an old dog new tricks" sounds like it applies here. There are a number of steps you can take:

The first is to accept that she won't change and that her purpose on earth is to behave immaturely. Think of it as a job with a quota: "Today she'll misbehave seven times." Then, if she reaches the goal, you've won your bet. If she fails to reach the quota, you win again. And if she exceeds her quota, that means you have to raise your expectations for tomorrow!

Part of what you and your colleagues have to do is take a serious look at how disruptive her behavior is to office productivity. If you can quantify the negative impact, perhaps it is worth discussing with HR or a higher level in the company hierarchy. If there are demonstrable data that her behavior is costing the company money/productivity, the decision-makers need to know about it.

If increased office tension is one of the more egregious side-effects of her presence, perhaps the people who are being bothered by her could get together during breaks, after work, or whenever it is appropriate to enjoy yourselves without her. Ignoring her, if it does not cut into productivity, can give you the freedom to derive more enjoyment from work.

A more humane approach could be to try to discover her interests outside of work, or any problems she's dealing with (family issues, health or financial problems, nasty neighbors, and so on). Figure out whether giving her a chance to air her grievances might help reduce the tension she feels as well as the tension she brings into the workplace. Maybe she needs a friend or confidante. Just treating her as a grumpy old lady demeans her; she may be a complicated or even interesting person. Perhaps her taste in music, books, movies, sports, or whatever can become a common topic. There may be non-work issues that bring her together with at least some of the rest of the group.

---

## Dealing With Nasty Negotiators

### From: Joe, Harare, Zimbabwe

**Question:** *How should one handle unprincipled and unethical negotiators?*

**Response:** When you run up against unprincipled or unethical negotiators (notice I said "when" and not "if"), the first question you should ask is whether you really have to negotiate with them or if you have a BATNA, a Best Alternative to a Negotiated Agreement. In this case, your BATNA could be to negotiate with someone else or find a solution to your concern using assets under your own control.

If you *must* deal with nasty negotiators, however, you need to do as much preparation as possible. You should consider your objectives and give thought to the idea that "winning" may really be a matter of minimizing your losses. In addition, you should learn as much as you can about the interests of the nasty negotiator to see what you have to offer him that makes him need you. The more he needs you, the stronger your BATNA. You should try to find out about him and his interests through research with other people who know or deal with him, as well as by asking him lots of questions during the negotiation process.

There's a story that illustrates this point. During the late 19th-century in England, Lord Gladstone and Benjamin Disraeli were political rivals. There was controversy among the populace as to which man was the greatest in the British Empire. A woman learned that she was to be seated between Gladstone and Disraeli at a major banquet. Her friends asked her to decide, based on dinner conversation, which man was the greater. Upon her return she told her friends, "First I had a wonderful conversation with the brilliant Lord Gladstone. From what he told me about himself, I concluded he is the greatest man in the Empire. Then I turned my attention to Mr. Disraeli, who focused on learning about me. After that conversation, I realized that I am the finest woman in all Christendom!"

Listening to everyone, even "nasty negotiators," is a crucial technique. The clearer your understanding of where they are coming from, the greater the likelihood you'll find a route to an acceptable agreement.

If this nasty negotiator keeps trying to bully you into agreement, respond with silence. Keep a poker face, revealing nothing. He may get the message that his approach is not being received favorably—and perhaps that can open a door, as well.

## Do I Have to Go Along to Get Along?

### From: Christine, Parma, Ohio

**Question:** *I work with a doctor who is arrogant, extremely impatient, and rude. He makes snide remarks and constantly rolls his eyes. I have not worked with him long, but I understand he is like this with all the nurses and techs he works with.*

*I don't know how to deal with someone like this. It makes me angry that he treats people like this and at the same time makes me feel so down. I was told to not let him bother me and to ignore what he does or says. It's like everybody kisses his butt. Please help me.*

**Response:** You need to take a look at your alternatives in this situation. If you tell the doctor that his behavior interferes with the quality of care your group can provide patients, what is the worst he can do? If he can get you fired, how is the job market in your area for someone with your qualifications? Are alternative workplaces more attractive than your current one?

There are several approaches you can take; the most important rule is not to say (or even imply) to this particular doctor or anyone else you find annoying or difficult, "You are a bad person." That kind of statement is guaranteed to either escalate the unpleasantness or reduce your ability to influence the troublesome person. Instead, you can take the approach of describing your own response to the situation: "When someone says that to me, it undermines my self-confidence and makes me question whether I'm in the right profession, in the right workplace, working with the right people." Without pointing your finger at the offensive doctor, you are letting him know he is getting to you and that you are considering your alternatives.

Another approach is not to talk about yourself, but rather to ask the doctor questions about his behavior and intentions: "What do you mean by that?" "Why did you just roll your eyes?" "What effect do you hope to have on my job performance when you talk like that?"

Your colleagues who advised you to keep your head down and roll with the punches are *enablers* (a term most often used in situations of addiction and/or codependency). They are enabling the doctor to get away with unacceptable and inappropriate behavior. They have no right to complain about his behavior unless they are willing to make a concerted effort to let him know that the behavior is subverting the quality of the workplace and, most likely, the quality of their work, as well. You need to "inoculate" yourself against unpleasant surprises by understanding your BATNA and acting accordingly. You need to decide what steps you can take on your own. And you need to bring your colleagues into the situation as adults who have a right to be treated with respect, or who deserve no respect because they don't demand it.

One thing your question does not indicate is whether this environment is centered on one particular doctor or whether you are part of a larger organization, in which case you would have people further up the hierarchy to turn to. You should monitor the doctor's behavior toward his patients. If he shows them the same lack of respect, that can be harmful to your organization.

People who behave like the doctor you describe are more than likely very insecure. By disrespecting others, they are defending their own vulnerability. Do some research to figure out why this doctor's self-image is so weak. You never know how this information might help you cope with his obnoxiousness or find a way to get through his defenses to get him to behave like a civilized person.

---

## I Can't Get Through When He's Yelling

### From: Jackie, Boston, Massachusetts

**Question:** *How do you negotiate with someone in a work relationship who yells to get his point across and won't let you get a word in edgewise?*

**Response:** Someone who yells instead of engaging in civilized negotiation can drive you crazy. But it is not a hopeless situation.

First you always have to ask yourself, "Do I really need to deal with this person?" Assuming the answer is yes, there are steps you can take:

- Listen hard to the substance of what the "yeller" is saying. He may be expressing deep feelings or revealing very significant interests.

- Don't respond immediately. One possibility is to sit there with a poker face in absolute silence. In effect this is letting him know that what he said, or, more specifically, how he said it, is offensive or troublesome to you.

- Another response is to talk in a very soft voice. Speak very slowly. Make him listen to you, even to the point where he asks you to please speak a little louder. Your response should begin with an indication that you were listening: "If I understood you correctly, you just said...." Remember that while you may understand what he said, that doesn't necessarily mean you agree with it. Make that point clearly.

- If the yelling produces an emotional reaction in you, you might say, "When someone yells at me I feel hurt/insulted/misunderstood/as if we are not communicating"

When someone yells at you, it is reasonable to say—very gently—that you do not have a hearing problem but that you are interested in what is being said. This is also a time to take a deep breath, give yourself time to think, and find a creative, unexpected way to respond. A surprise often throws a "yeller" off-kilter, making him consider ideas that may not have occurred to him initially.

Yelling is an offensive form of misbehavior in many cultures, and a sign that the "yeller" is insecure about his capacity to influence other people in a rational way. If you respond rationally and intelligently, it may change the dynamics of the interaction.

# I Rear-ended His Car, but He Stayed Anonymous

## From: Marie, Ottawa, Canada

**Question:** *I was driving down the street when the car ahead of me suddenly braked. I slammed on my brakes a little too late and lightly bumped into the back bumper. There is no damage to either car.*

*The man insisted on taking my insurance information but did not ask for anything else (for example, my license), and he refused to give me his insurance information. The police were not called and no report was made. As I am a young female I felt quite intimidated by the whole thing. I do not understand what to make of all of this; as I said, there was no damage. I live in Canada and he is from the United States. What are your thoughts?*

**Response:** It sounds as though there are two different issues here. The simpler one is the issue of the exchange of information. If you kept a record of his license plate number, as well as which U.S. state issued the license plate, it should not be difficult for your insurance agent to find out who owns the car you bumped into. You should ask your agent whether there is any need to file a report with the agent or any law enforcement agency.

The more serious issue is that you felt intimidated because you are a young female. Almost everyone has had a conversation or confrontation and then thought of the perfect rejoinder or comeback only *after* it was over. Your first action should have been to face your situation head-on and say to yourself, *I am a young female, but I have an obligation to stand up for myself. No other person—male or female, large or small—is entitled to treat me disrespectfully.* You are lucky that you have an opportunity to reflect on this lesson in a situation in which everything—and everyone—appears to have emerged unscathed. After this, you should remember to go through a checklist of what to say or do (or what not to say or do) when faced by a potentially intimidating person.

In the case of your minor collision, you had an opportunity to negotiate in the simplest form. You could have offered to bargain with the other driver: "If you will give me your insurance information [and whatever other information you consider important], I will reciprocate by providing my information to you."

Think of your confrontations with difficult or intimidating people as an opportunity to trade with them. In this case you might have traded information. In another it may be a matter of trading civil behavior: "If you insist on treating me as a dumb young kid, I am afraid that we have nothing to discuss. If you treat me as you would want to be treated yourself, I would be pleased to reciprocate."

Remember that you have to pay attention to your own interests first; only then will you be able to judge whether your response to another person's demands make sense for you or are contrary to your interests.

Talk to other young women and friends about how they deal with intimidating people. Develop a checklist that each of you goes through in your mind when a potentially problematic situation crops up suddenly. If you rehearse how to respond, your response will be far more effective in the moment.

---

## They're Older, but Does That Make Them Right?

### From: Ariana, Kuala Lumpur, Malaysia

**Question:** *How should I deal with older people who stubbornly insist that they are always right?*

**Response:** Being stubborn and insisting one is right is not just a characteristic one finds in older people. People who insist they're right, who effectively say "my way or the highway," are taking a positional approach to negotiation. They are adopting a position, insisting their answer is the only one.

The basic problem here is that if they change their mind, they run the risk of losing face. In certain situations (for example, in certain cultures or companies), age can sometimes give someone an edge in terms of deserving deference. This can create an even more difficult situation when it comes to dealing with stubborn negotiators to whom deference is due.

If you need to reach an agreement with someone who takes a position, even if it is complicated by social rules, you need to ask as many questions as you can to accomplish two goals: to demonstrate that you are interested in and respectful of their opinion, and to give you a clearer understanding of why they've adopted their stubborn position.

Sometimes you are dealing with people who've had more experience than you, and learning from that experience can help you find a more effective way of connecting with them and influencing their thinking. Often people are threatened by others who have contrary ideas; it can cause them to lose face, to lose the benefits of social or professional authority, and to feel pain in their ego.

Finding out why someone has adopted a position is crucial. If they are saving their "face," you have to find ways to help them change their position without looking as if they are giving in to your pressure. If they think they have the only answer, due to their knowledge or experience, if you learn more about their interests and objectives, you may be able to prove that an alternative to the approach they have adopted will yield better results for them.

In all of this, you need to monitor your own motives. Are you trying to reach an agreement that maximizes the benefits to the negotiating parties, or are you trying to prove something about your own power? Think about the price each party might have to pay by changing his/her way of dealing with an issue. Figure out who has more to gain by flexibility, both in the short term and in the long term.

---

## She Says No
## Before I Can Finish My Sentence

### From: Joke, Leiden, Netherlands

**Question:** *I am a manager in a facility department. One of the workers leads the IT section (the help desk). She is being supervised by the director (my boss) and doesn't want to deal with me in any way. The person who had my job before me let this happen.*

*She is glad to have the director as her supervisor, because this gives her credit and power with her clients. She is "difficult" in the sense that she is afraid of anyone dealing with "her" tasks or job. She defends her tasks and her section like a lioness. Everyone who tries to oppose her views is regarded as an enemy. And to each new proposal, she says (before you have ended your sentence) no. She is doing her work appropriately, but could achieve more if she were more willing to listen.*

*I have not decided what to do. If I try to force her to accept my management, I don't think I win a lot by doing that; however, the director would be glad if I did so. On the other hand, if I don't do anything, she will be out of my way. While this could make my life easier, it is no good for the department as a whole.*

*Her ways of communicating are repulsive to me: she doesn't listen, she repeats herself, she says no, hides facts from me, and the list goes on. So I don't like her very much at this moment. What can I do?*

**Response:** It is unfortunate that your predecessor allowed this situation to develop. I wonder if his/her predecessor did things the same way. It is also unfortunate that your supervisor is willing to allow the situation to remain unchanged; it means your boss is failing to delegate part of your job to you and, as a consequence, is both undercutting your authority and reducing the productivity of your department.

You need to take a look at the priorities involved. Are there ways of measuring how this woman's difficult behavior costs the company productivity and therefore money? Can you present this to your boss and ask him whether he is satisfied with the situation? If your boss wants to have this woman report directly to him, you should ask the boss to make that a formal decision so that you can say (to yourself, at least), *Well, I've finally gotten rid of her.*

You should do some homework: What has been this woman's history in the company? What kind of relationships does she have with other colleagues, with the people she supervises, with outside clients/customers/suppliers? Is there something in her personal history that makes her so insecure that she feels she must behave like the lioness you describe? In addition to satisfying her ego, what else does she have to gain by maintaining her bad attitude and refusing to be managed by you?

The more you learn about what she finds important and who she takes seriously, the greater the likelihood you will be able to analyze her behavior and respond optimally. It may be that as you get to know more about her, there may be some minor areas of agreement upon which you and she can build and begin to treat each other in a civilized manner.

It's critical to remember that, at least as you present the situation, every time she drives you crazy, she wins and you lose. Whenever you are compelled to deal with her, you should expect extremely bad behavior, and when she behaves badly, you should laugh to yourself, *There, I knew she would do that.* If you take that approach and create an expectation in yourself that she will be a problem, every time she fulfills that prophecy, you can congratulate yourself on winning your bet. For example, you may tell yourself, *When I say [x], I bet it will take her seven seconds to say no.* Then you can keep an eye on her and see how good your prediction was. If it becomes a game to you, that's somewhat less stressful than a constant war.

Ultimately you need to find a way to restructure the relationship. Unless she is motivated to do so, as well, it won't work. After you have done all the homework you can in terms of cost/benefit analysis, relationship history, and other relevant facts, you must have an honest conversation with your supervisor. Do not approach the supervisor as a victim of this woman; rather, approach the boss as a manager who is looking to his supervisor as a leader who can provide guidance for the good of the department, the company, and the people he supervises.

---

## Dealing With Dirty Tricks

### From: Angernie, Queensland, Australia

**Question:** *I need some negotiation advice on how to deal with dirty tricks during purchases and sales.*

**Response:** Recognizing when people are attempting to use dirty tricks is the most important part of the process. If you spot a dirty trick during negotiation, it is your job to call attention to your awareness of what is going on. Don't say, "You're a bad guy trying to play a dirty trick on me." A far more effective approach is to say, "I have the feeling that something strange is happening here. Could you explain what you mean when you say [x]?" What you need to do is call attention to the fact that you are paying attention to the negotiation and that attempted tricks are not going to fool you. If you are not judgmental, at least at first, you give the other person a chance to clean up her act and negotiate more fairly. This can set the tone for better negotiation practices as the process goes forward.

Very often we discover the dirty tricks only *after* the negotiations are over. If we have been tricked into a bad deal, we can contact the other party and say, "If I had known that this presented inaccurately, I would have made a different decision. As it is, I feel trapped in a bad deal with you. If you are willing to reopen discussions, this will help improve the present deal and increase the likelihood that our future dealings will be more satisfactory." You want to call attention to the value of improving the long-term relationship.

Sometimes the trickster doesn't care. She is risking the long-term relationship with you as well as her reputation for fairness and honesty. In those cases, you may have to live with the consequences of having agreed to a bad deal. But you have also gained the knowledge of how dirty tricks are used; you can treat the experience as part of your learning process. It is a frustrating position in which to find yourself, but since it strengthens you for the future, it can have long-term benefits.

It happens to everyone—hopefully only once. As the saying goes, if you cheat me once, shame on you; if you cheat me twice, shame on me. Learn from your experience and you'll keep getting better and better.

---

## What Makes a Person Difficult?

### From: Elyse, Vancouver, British Columbia

**Question 1:** *What do you think makes a coworker, or people in general, "difficult" (or at least appear difficult)? What is really happening in these situations? Are there different ways of looking at it? Is perspective important?*

**Response 1:** Someone may seem difficult for multiple reasons. He may present a bottleneck in the decision-making process; he may be so insecure (as an individual or as a member of an organization) that he feels compelled to act aggressively because he confuses aggression with assertiveness; or he may just be genuinely disinclined to treat you properly/politely.

My favorite definition of a bureaucrat is "someone whose entire self-definition is based on his or her power to say no." When you run across someone like that, the bottleneck type, dealing with him may not be the answer. It could make a lot more sense to try to deal with the problem, the issue at hand. If you focus on solving the problem, you may find that the bottleneck really isn't a necessary part of the critical path you must take to reach a positive result. Bottom line: try to figure out whether there is an alternative route.

People who are insecure often feel that no one understands them. In these instances, paying attention to them, finding out what makes them tick, discovering what motivates them, can help you find ways to turn them into collaborators rather than obstacles. Listen to them. Take them seriously. Treat them with respect and interest. It can change the dynamic of the relationship.

**Question 2:** *Why do you think it's important to learn how to deal with difficult coworkers? What are the advantages of such a skill?*

**Response 2:** The basic reason for learning how to deal with difficult coworkers is that it will keep you from going crazy. If you can develop perspective and a strategy for dealing with them, you are also more likely to accomplish your objectives.

In dealing with difficult people, you want to separate the people from the problem. Asking whether the problem would go away if that difficult so-and-so were to jump into the harbor wearing cement shoes may give you a clearer perspective of what has to be done.

Dealing with difficult people also forces you to practice self-discipline. For example, one crucial rule is that only one person can get angry at a time. If you can hold your temper, at least you have earned the reward of being able to congratulate yourself on what a wonderful, strong, in-control person you are. That may not solve the problem, but at least it helps you feel good about yourself.

One other result/advantage is that it helps to clarify your objectives. Sometimes "winning" really means "minimizing your losses." Knowing someone is difficult gives you a better sense of what you can expect, and doing a successful reality check of your expectations can give you considerable power.

**Question 3:** *What do you consider to be the fundamental steps in communicating with a difficult person? What should one do before, during, and after? Are there any specific questions to ask, patterns to follow?*

**Response 3:** While it is dangerous to think there are always specific steps you *must* follow, it can make sense to think in terms of a few. Prepare yourself and do your homework. Ask questions about why each of you wants what you want. Figure out whether you are really compelled to work with this person or whether you have an alternative.

Another step to take is to listen carefully to the difficult person. You learn more with your mouth closed and your ears open. Think of the initial phase of the negotiation as an opportunity to check the assumptions you made in your preparation, and a chance to learn more about what approaches are likely to get the other party to respond favorably.

The last step I'll mention here is to consider the priorities involved. What are your long-term interests? How important is this particular relationship to you? Is the process proceeding fairly? Are you dealing with someone who can really deliver on the decisions he or she makes?

**Question 4:** *In my research, discussions of so-called difficult people usually break them down into behavioral or personality types. What are some of the more common "types" of people that are often cited as being difficult? What makes them difficult? What are they really trying to achieve with their behaviors? If you don't ascribe to this "type" theory, perhaps just focus on behaviors rather than personalities (since any combination of behaviors can make up a personality). Finally, what should be one's action plan in dealing with these types?*

**Response 4:** I do have a problem with the idea of types, because everyone interacts differently with different people (or different "types," if you will). Clearly, there exist some psychological profiles that describe people who are best avoided. However, even here it is possible that some people thrive on interacting with them. Difficult personalities need to be examined in terms of what they have to offer, from both positive and negative standpoints. Again, separating the person from the substantive issue needing a solution is the most effective way to make progress.

We are all put off by certain behaviors. If people refuse to respond, if they won't look us in the eye, if they ignore our existence—that can be a bummer. On the other hand, in some cultures, these may be normal behaviors, so we take a big risk if we assume that people are knowingly trying to offend us. Our job is to call attention to things that bother us. We can't point the finger and accuse someone of being difficult. Rather, it makes more sense to say something along the lines of, "When people don't look me in the eye, it makes me feel uneasy." After all, we may have habits that drive other people nuts, and unless they tell us, we may never know.

There is one other factor to consider. If you are one of the many people who find a particular person a problem, perhaps everyone so aggrieved should discuss things together and figure out how to heal their relationship with the difficult person. Treating him with more respect and/or taking his concerns seriously may help turn things around. If that doesn't work, it may make sense to look for ways around him, to marginalize him so he is "dethroned" from his pivotal place in the process.

Don't forget: you can fight fires without burning bridges.

---

## Reconciling People After a Civil War

### From: Oliver, Pietmaritzburg, South Africa

**Question:** *I am a Liberian student attending college in South Africa. Two years ago, I was in Liberia during the 14 years of civil war. Relatives, brothers, and sisters were fighting among themselves. The crisis left 300,000 people dead. I am hoping to return home someday and help the people I know reconcile with one another. The war has caused lasting bitterness within families. Steve, what can I do to reconcile these people?*

**Response:** The bitterness in war's aftermath can be overwhelming, whether it has been a civil war, an insurgency, or a war between nations. To a certain extent there are some advantages once a civil war has ended; the people who have been on opposing sides remain in place. Remaining in proximity with folks who were on the other side more or less forces the former enemies to find ways to live together—at first, simply by not harming each other, and then later, by dealing with issues of commerce, education, and other activities where there can be shared objectives. With careful effort it may be possible to help members of divided families or communities recognize the value of focusing on the future.

In negotiation, the past has no future. One cannot change what has happened; and it is virtually impossible to change a person's view of history, particularly if it has left bitterness or pain in his or her heart. However, efforts to get people to focus on how they want the future to look may yield potential areas of agreement. For example, virtually everyone wants safe drinking water, a good healthcare system, and a reasonably orderly society in which it is possible to live and work and have a good life.

Trying to reach agreement on small portions of those large interests may give people who carry grudges against each other a reason to work together without committing themselves to becoming pals. Ideally, working together to achieve mutually agreed-upon objectives can give people the opportunity to see one another as human beings again, as subjects to be treated with a modicum of respect, rather than as objects to be ignored or mistreated. Perhaps down the road, mutual tolerance can result, and, ultimately, friendship may become possible.

Another step you can take is to look for individuals who are respected by people from both sides of the conflict. Religious leaders, businesspeople who have a reputation for treating everyone fairly, and medical professionals who have no politics when they deal with patients are all examples of the kind of people who might have the capacity to overcome grudges. Within families, there may be shared interests in pleasing elders, developing relationships with people who marry in, or giving support and affection to newborn babies.

Sports and other forms of entertainment can be used within a reasonably sized community to bring people back together. For example, when forming a football team, don't let each team represent one of the sides in the civil war. Mix the players together so that each team is its own group and not a mechanism to continue the conflict vicariously. Similarly, musical groups that include performers from formerly opposed groups may give people a chance to act in concert rather than dissonance.

The bottom line is that this issue does not lend itself to grand gestures. "One person at a time" should be the aim in order to maximize the impact of a peacemaker's efforts. The idea is not to create an objective that could be blown away (literally and figuratively) if factions develop when the peacemaker tries too hard to accomplish too much, too fast.

Waging war takes planning and involves appalling behavior. Waging peace takes diplomacy, thought, and tenacity of spirit. I wish you good luck, a steadfast heart, and the capacity to think and act creatively to deal with the situation.

# Epilogue

This book is built on questions: questions from real people all around the world. The advice it contains can bring sense to your efforts to solve all different kinds of problems in cooperation with others.

Negotiation is a process by which people exchange things of value in a civilized manner. Value is rarely simply about money, however; what people are looking for is something that's a good fit for their interests. The one commodity that is exchanged in every single negotiation is *information*. Generally, the information you exchange tells you whether what another party has to offer us will help you meet your own interests. When you listen attentively, you're more likely to learn what it will take to convince others to agree with you. Sometimes the information you uncover will give you a reason to walk away, but being empowered to do that strengthens you as an individual and will force you to question whether there is a better way to go forward.

The name of my company's flagship training program is "Fighting Fires Without Burning Bridges." Our aim is to help people see that negotiation is not a one-off process, but rather an episode in an ongoing relationship. Most of the time we negotiate with the same people again and again; but even if we're bargaining as shoppers in a distant marketplace, how we treat our negotiation partners is a reflection of who we are.

As you have seen, *The Practical Negotiator* is not designed to come to a single, neat conclusion. I encourage you to let your mind move outside of the box in your approach to problem-solving. Simply being creative is not likely to yield miraculous personality changes; nevertheless, you will, I hope, be empowered and better prepared to own your behavior and your strategy. As you develop your negotiation strategy, the more questions you ask, the more empowered you will be to negotiate wisely and effectively. Remember, there is no such thing as a stupid question. But also remember there can be stupid answers. Always focus on asking questions that will yield useful information, and don't ever answer without giving some thought to the potential range of consequences your answer may yield. *Think fast, talk slow.*

Hopefully this book has helped humanize negotiation for you. I have certainly found the process a wonderful way to learn about others—and myself.

# Index

# About the Author

Steven P. Cohen is a native of Boston who has also lived in New York, Buffalo, Washington, London, and Paris. President of The Negotiation Skills Company, Inc., he is a graduate of Columbia Law School, Brandeis University, and Henley Management College.

Following law school, Mr. Cohen spent a dozen years in politics and government, including service as the City of Boston's Washington Lobbyist during the Nixon and Ford Administrations, a job which required considerable negotiation skill. His subsequent career in commercial real estate development and management added further depth to his negotiation experience.

He has worked as a negotiation consultant to hundreds of companies and government agencies in more than 20 countries, engaged in banking, healthcare, insurance, management consulting, international law, logistics, heavy manufacturing, and energy production. Some of his better-known clients include Wal-Mart, General Motors, the UK's National Health Service, Flextronics, BP, Maersk, Siemens, Total, British Telecom, Linklaters, Proudfoot, and Taj Hotels.

A visiting business school professor for more than 10 years (each) at Groupe HEC (Paris) and Brandeis University's International Business

School, as well as at other business schools in the United States, the UK, France, Spain, Portugal, and Russia, Mr. Cohen has worked with people from more than 85 countries. His previous book, *Negotiating Skills for Managers* (McGraw-Hill), has been published in seven international editions.

He and his wife, Andréa MacLeod, have two daughters, one grandson, and, as of this writing, high hopes for more grandchildren.